LETS GO Databas

The AS/400 & IBM i Pocket Database Guide

QuikCourse: Query/400 By Example

by Brian W. Kelly

– A Comprehensive Book of DB2/400 examples & information for the new Query User –

This book is based on The AS/400 Database DB2/400 and the excellent Kelly Consulting QuikCourse™ classroom education modules.

LETS GO PUBLISH

Contains significant reference material, how-to's, and insightful tutorials.

Published by: LETS GO PUBLISH!
Brian P. Kelly, Publisher
P.O Box 621
Wilkes-Barre PA 18703
www.letsgopublish.com
Library of Congress Copyright Information Pending
ISBN #   **978-0-9980848-9-3**

Publishing dates: 2006, 2016

Price $19.99 USD

10   9   8   7   6   5   4   3   2   1

Dedication

To the most popular IBM Database of all time. Without IBM's free Database for AS/400 and IBM i, there would be lots of missing information in the world.

Acknowledgments

These acknowledgments are copied from the 2006 version of this book. An updated version of the acknowledgments is at www.letsgopublish.com. Look for acknowledgments on left menu. Query acknowledgments were originally written in 2002 and then updated with the code in 2006. The acknowledgments are printed here as they existed in 2006. As then, they are very sincere.

Please note that since her eminence, Wiley Ky Eyely, a recent friend of a publishing magnate was not yet born at this time in 2006, we defer respectfully to the online version of the acknowledgments for her individual kudos, with full deference to Ms. Ky Eyely.

I would like to thank many people for helping me in this effort.

I would first like to thank my immediate family, starting with my lovely and dear wife, Patricia. Again, as I offer in all my books, my wife Patricia is my source. She is the person who keeps me alive and sane and well—in more ways than can be mentioned. She is the glue that holds our whole family together. Besides that, she keeps getting better looking as the years go by, and I love to see her wonderful face every day in my life. Thank you God for that!

Her daddy, a wonderful man in his own right, Smokey Piotroski, called his little girl Packy as a nickname. Though Stash is now with the Angels, I love that name and the person who wears it and I still use it to address my little Packy. God gave me a gift that keeps me going. Thank you Packy for all you do to keep me and our whole family well and mostly, thank you for the smile that you always put on my face.

I would also like to thank my twenty-one year-old daughter, Katie, who is still my little baby doll. Kate helps me in any way she can. Even more than that, her sweet voice and her accomplished guitar playing gets the muse racing as my fingers pound the keyboard. Katie is starting to feel better now and we thank God for that but it still is not easy for her. She is on her way to being OK. I thank my Katie for she will always be Daddy's Little Girl. I love you very much. A special thank you also goes to Dr. Patrick Kerrigan, the consummate physician and good friend of our family. Dr. Kerrigan is working his way up the list in record time. Dr. Patrick comes to the job with the abilities of Hippocrates and the patience of Job. He has left no stone unturned in helping Katie through her illness, and his work continues as a solution is on its way.

Thanks also go out to my twenty-four year-old son, Michael, who more than made the dean's list in his last semester at King's College this year as he received his B.S. Degree in Accounting. Michael had very good LSATs and his academic record was more than enough for him to be accepted in Law School and he will be beginning his three year trek this month. I am always happy to have my youngest son close by so I am going to miss him very much.

I also thank my twenty-five-year-old son, Brian, who edits and publishes many of my books. He is an astute grammarian and a prolific writer in his own right. He just knocked 'em dead recently in Law School and graduated Magna Cum Laude.

Brian spent a few months taking courses in preparation for the Bar Examination, which he passed no sweat on the first try. After a short break, Brian will be starting a clerkship. Congratulations Brian, you make us very proud. Mom and I are very proud of all of our children and we thank each of them for their work in academia and their efforts on our behalf.

Thanks also to the extended family who are always there to lend a helping hand. Barb, Kim & Dave, Dawn, Cindy & Dave Boyle, Megan and Sean are some of the most wonderful family in my life. And dad Joe, with the angels, always gets his plugs in. Thanks also to Melissa and Paul Sabol and their new baby boy Paul IV. Crocodile Dundee Sabol and the Plains Police

Department are always there to make sure all the families are safe.

Accomplishments often materialize because of a strong friendship infrastructure. I am pleased to have a number of great friends. Among them is my longtime best friend Dennis Grimes, who is always there to help, though he may think everything I write sounds the same. Professor Grimes is on the faculty with me at Marywood University and he is a CIO for Klein Wholesale.

He is very talented and very helpful. Many of his quips and quotes find their way into my writing. Barbara Grimes, Patricia Grimes Yencha, Elizabeth (Wizzler), Mary the PhD., Denyse back from the U.K., Grandma Viola, and Grandma Gert also pitch in whenever the opportunity arises. Dennis helps me in whatever way I ask, especially when I am stuck. I really appreciate all you do for me "D." Thank you

The busiest guy on all of my book projects, besides myself, has always been Joe McDonald. Joe is the businessman in our publishing venture, and in that, he's all business. Joe is the former Publisher of the Scranton Tribune/Scrantonian Newspaper. So he's got the right background to make sure everything is A-OK! Our next book is not going to be technical as we are moving the publishing business to include children's books and third party authors.

Joe assures me that after this book's second printing, he will have the courage to lead me to the children's side of the business where our next book is scheduled to be The Adventures of Eddy (The Dog) written by Joe's Grandson. Soon, it will be on the bookshelves of America. My thanks also go to Peg McDonald for making sure that Joe is always ready for action.

Of course, the long list of helping hands contains lots of names: Gerry Rodski and his wonderful friend-- Joyce, Jeanne and

Farmer Joe Elinsky, John and Carol Anstett, Grandma Leona and Grandma Annie (from Mayflower), Carolyn and Joe Langan, Bob & Cathy Wood, Karen and Al Komorek (Al was alive when this was written originally], Joe and Betta Demmick, Bonnie and George Mohanco, Becker and Robin Mohanco, Lilya, Josh, and Alaina Like Mohanco, Bob and Nettie Lussi, Kim and Ruth Borland--- they are all there when needed..

Other helping hands include Dr. Lou and Marie Guarnieri as well as Mary and Cindy Guarnieri, whose hands have been indispensable. I can't forget Mike and Frannie Kurilla & Frankie and Tony, Jerry and Hedy Cybulski, Linda DeBoo and Bob Buynak, Joe, the Chief, LaSarge, John and Susan Rose, and Dave and Nancy Books. Thanks also to Dr. Rex Dumdum from Marywood-- my academic mentor. Special thanks also to the E.L. Meyers Class of 1965 (40th reunion last year) for some early training in the art of writing.

And don't let me forget Patricia's parents, Arline and Stanley Piotroski, who continue to guide us in our lives. Cathy and Marty Piotroski, Dr. Susan Piotroski and Dr. Mitch Bornstein, Matt and Allie, Dr. Stan Piotroski, Carol Piotroski, Sister Marlene, Justin and Katie, Merek, MacKenzie, Myranda, Erin, Ralph Harvey, Lynn, and Scott Piotroski, Pierre Le Kep. The Kelly parents -- Ed and Irene also provide guidance from upstairs as well as direct intervention as needed; Anna Maye, Nancy and Angel Jim Flannery (Leland (No K) Zard), Renee (Bean), Jimmy (Jim Bob), Bridget, Mary (MeeWee), Danny, Michael (McPike) , Ken (La Rue), Jen, Angel David Davidow (Brunoch Zard), Stephen (P.Q. Whoozer), Matthew(M.Q. Peph), Bailee Roo, Viva La Vieve, and Billiard Peph, Joe and Rosalee, Raymond, Paula, and the real Sparkey. Mary and Bill Daniels, Liz (Weezler), Bri, Megan (Megeldeebaigledee), Bill Jr (Billdog) ., Vicky, Sophia (Chubby Cheeks,) Elise (La Leese), Diane and Joe Kelly, Tara and Col, Ed and Eudart Kelly, Eddie, John, and Robert. Bill Rolland- Notre Dame's # 1 Fan and master of accommodations, Bill Kustas, Bill & Helen Kush, Steve and Shelly Bartolomei, Keith and Dorie Zinn,

Cheryl Danowski, Ricky, Joane, Briana and Eric Bayer, Rick and Donna Pinkofski, and of course the great musical cutter Harrison Arthur and his friend Harry Heck Jr. More thanks to Judy Jones and Jerry Reisch and Judy Judy Judy Seroska.

[I know I have corrected many of the acknowledgement mistakes since this book was printed but this is the original. For the updates, please go to www.letsgopublish.com]

Going back to the top of the list of helpers is my wonderful and huge pack of cousins. The list begins with the Uncles and Aunts, many of whom are now Angels. Uncle Nick and Aunt Emma McKeown, Dave and Kathleen Conklin, Rita and Frank DeRiancho, Joan and Tom Nelson, Aunt Ruth and Uncle Joe McKeown, Kathy and Joe McKeown Jr., Aunt Louise and Uncle Jimmy McKeown, Patsy, Danny and Jerry McKeown, Nina and Jim Brady, Jimmy Brady, Tommy and Mary Rowan, Arlene and Richard May, Little Tommy Rowan, Helen and Joe Drexinger, and all the other cousins, uncles & aunts who can't make it to the special muse event every summer in Montrose.

Of course, there's Uncle Johnny Kelly, Aunt Catherine and Leonard Lamascola, Aunt Mary Kelly, Sharon, Maureen, Jud, Pat Jr., and Tommy Kelly. Red Cloud is also on the list for his due diligence in writing postcards.

In the special care category, Dr. Lou has been making sure that my bones are aligned properly for years. So that I can give those speeches with a bright smile, I got some big help from Dr. Lou Kicha the Great and his highly competent team of professionals at Aspen Dental-- John Cicon, Carol Kephart, Nicole Arnone, Anita Florek, and the tooth architect, Mary Lou Lennox. Thank you all very much.

Special acknowledgments to Steven Dressler and Howard Klein, the top management team at Klein Wholesale Distributors in Wilkes-Barre, PA, who use Query to the fullest. Their vision, foresight, and execution have brought Klein to the enviable position of being the third largest candy and tobacco wholesaler in the United States.

Various members of the Klein development staff offered information over the time in which this book was written. In alphabetical order, by first name, the Klein team includes: Barb Chaderton, Bill 'Curly' Kepics, Cindy Dorzinsky, Cindy Goodwin, Dennis Grimes, Eric Priest, Jeff Massaker, Jerry Reisch, Joe Byorick, Joe Rydzewski, John Robbins, Paula Terpak, Rod Smith, and Rosalind Robertson.

I would also like to thank Nancy Lavan, our sponsor at Offset Paperback, our printer [who guided all publishing efforts though we have chosen CreateSpace for this update.] She continually encourages us in our writing and publishing efforts. Chris Grieves, our new customer service person has made working with the printing process an easy task. Special thanks go to Michele Thomas, who takes ideas and makes wonderful images from them, such as this wonderful cover.

To sum up my acknowledgments, as I do in every book that I have written, I am compelled to offer that I am truly convinced that "the only thing you can do alone in life is fail." Thanks to my family, good friends, and a helping team, I was not alone.

Table of Contents

Preface:

This pocket guide introduces the notion of relational database for the AS/400 and IBM i developer, and perhaps more importantly, to the prospective developer. Yes, a non-AS/400 programmer can also use this book to gain a tremendous amount of insight into the following areas:

1. Relational database
2. DB2/400, the AS/400 and IBM i integrated native relational database management system
3. The native data definition and data manipulation language, which comes with all AS/400 and IBM i machines - DDS.

Since all applications start with data, this book is clearly designed from an AS/400 programmer's application development (AD) perspective.

Both entry level and existing programmers will enjoy the easy to read, down home style of this pocket guide. A general notion of how file systems work and / or how DBMS systems tick is certainly helpful. But, even if you are new to AS/400 and IBM i, and you want to understand how to use the native database for maintenance or for new applications, you can learn all you need right from this pocket book. It is written in a way which assumes very little prior database knowledge.

Though it may take a bit more than 24 hours for you to be designing major databases, you can gain the idea of how to get the job done, one project at a time, one example at a time, by using this pocket guide. You will learn about the file object in its physical and logical form, and how both forms can help you design and implement systems which provide productivity functions at the database and the program level.

This book consists of one of one large, reasonably comprehensive QuikCourse that describes the notion of database and the AS/400 & IBM I database implementations. It also teaches the developer how to program the database. The precursor modules in The Pocket Developers Guide were built to take a new developer to the AS/400 and IBM i and introduce her or him to all of the development tools in the IBM storehouse. This database book was originally intended to be a major QuikCourse in the newly released LETS GO PUBLISH AS/400 Pocket Developers' Guide (also by yours truly). It was just too big to include in its entirety.

I still refer to it as QuikCourse F. That's where it would have fit in the first pocket guide. At about 300 pages and 20 chapters, however, it was far too big to condense to one chapter. Instead, it is all contained within this book. The fact is that you really can't develop, and you can't program, without being able to build databases to store your application's data. So, you should consider this book as a necessary part of your IBM i education.

This Database QuikCourse is designed to make it easy for you to learn the native AS/400 and IBM i database facilities from file objects to access paths to coding DDS. As a database QuikCourse, this module originally was a two-day standup formal classroom course. It was designed with slides and notes for stand-up instruction. It is the direct result of its conversion to a stand-alone lecture / tutorial / reference format with plenty of action and plenty of examples. For those interested in SQL, there is a Pocket Developers Guide for SQL that is available in the series.

You can learn the IBM i database just by reading this book. All of the material from the database course is in here. But, if you can convince your systems administrator to give you some real authority, you can do even more. You can practice by typing in the small sets of DDS code snippets. In the process you can actually build the same databases that you see in the examples. Then, you can use the Pocket Developers' Guide to learn DFU so that you can enter data into your files. You can use the Query Developers Guide then to print reports from your new databases. You can also use the SQL guide to run Select, Insert, and Update statements against your newly created DBs.

There is no CD. In the classroom course there was no CD. You can type in these small sets of DDS and observe the full database process. Practice makes perfect. There's not a lot of keying, since the examples are all small. After a few statements, you'll be building IBM i file objects.

Go ahead and leaf through this book now. You'll see it is chocked full of examples. Many screen shots are included so you can play along with your AS/400 or IBM i server.

Who Should Read this book?

New programmers, existing programmers, supervisors, operation personnel, and advanced end users should all take this overgrown QuikCourse — or a selection of chapters made by IT management. In fact, IT management should consider reading or browsing this whole book to better understand how to match personnel with the areas of database study included in this QuikCourse.

IT managers need to consider educating programmers in database techniques. The fact is that many requirements can be met with just a few extra database statements. Database knowledge can save a wealth of high level language (HLL) coding.

If you plan to train operations people or PC people as AS/400 developers, or you want to help your staff better understand the marvels of the IBM i integrated database, this is the right book for you.

With all of the smart, yet sometimes clueless PC technicians running around every business and institution, there are many who would appreciate the opportunity to learn the AS/400 native database and who would do well if redeployed. I've even seen smart shipping clerks become programmers in a few months. This book and others in the series can be all you need to move them off the mark. This is the way to learn IBM I database.

If you are an IT Shop manager, and you've always wanted to be able to tell your team what you know about database on the AS/400 and IBM i, but you did not have the time, I've done it for you. I've said what you would have said if you had the time to say it Moreover, the folks at LETS GO PUBLISH! think you'll like what you would have said.

Consider creating a home-made programmer with some nice database knowledge. It may be a good deal for you and for your company. Like everything in our industry, all you need to do to succeed is be smart and work hard. If you think you need hands on help, send an email to Kelly Consulting and we'd be glad to help.

The Step Often Forgotten

It helps to remember that before anybody can work on their first program at your shop, they have to understand the AD environment and the tools that are in the shop's development kit. The next thing they need to know is how the database works. That's how we once taught formal development and database courses. We still do it that way when asked.

First the AD tools; then the database. By supplying sample databases and plenty of examples in this QuikCourse, this DB Pocket Guide can prepare your team to effectively engage the AS/400 and IBM i database without spending thousands of dollars on computer based training or classroom education. I'll miss you in my classes but you will learn regardless. Invite me to your shop for a Q & A. after the learning.

When prospective developers learn the AD tools, and the database, they can then move on to learning or using your AS/400 or IBM I programming languages such as RPG/400, ILE RPG (RPGIV), CL and even COBOL. Unfortunately, most IT shops do it the other way around. The student is sent to programming school or assigned to a real project long before he or she learns the IBM i system, the system's essential AD tools, and the database. This book can help you get things done in the right sequence.

We wish you well in your database endeavors, and we hope to see you again reading our next book in this series: The IBM i Pocket Query Guide.

Brian W. Kelly
Wilkes-Barre, Pennsylvania

About the Author

Brian W. Kelly is a retired Assistant Professor in the Business Information Technology (BIT) program at Marywood University, where he also served as the IBM i and midrange systems technical advisor to the IT faculty. Kelly developed and taught many college and professional courses in the IT and business areas. He is also a contributing technical editor to IT Jungle's "The Four Hundred" and "Four Hundred Guru" Newsletters.

A former IBM Senior Systems Engineer, he has an active consultancy in the information technology field, (www.kellyconsulting.com). He is the author of 87 books and numerous articles (hundreds) about current IT topics. Kelly is a frequent speaker at COMMON, IBM conferences, and other technical conferences and user group meetings across the United States. His favorite COMMON speaker was his buddy, the late Al Barsa Jr., one of the best ever.

Though much of this book was conceived and some of it was published before today, publishing standards groups acknowledge this as Brian Kelly's 87th book. Thank you for the great support of Kelly's technical books from John Wiley, Cardinal Business Media, IT Jungle, MC Press, 29th Street Press as well as the many seminars Mr. Kelly taught over the years.

I think Brian looks lots younger than 68 in this pic. Don't you think?

QuikCourse F.

AS/400 and IBM i Database Concepts and DDS Coding

Chapter 1. What is a Database?

The Database Concept

Before we get into the AS/400 database specifically, let's examine the notion of a database and relational database, in particular.

Data can be defined simply as a group of unorganized facts. For emphasis, many use the redundant term "raw data" to refer to "data" to accentuate the unorganized nature of the facts. Information, a term often misused in place of data, is data, organized for decision making. Through computer processes and database structures, data becomes information.

A database then is an organized collection of data (information) that is necessary to perform a task or application. Related data fields are grouped together into a format called a record. Similar records are grouped together into a file. One or more related data files can be grouped to make up a data base. What is Data Base Management?

Data Base Management is the process of managing data. It is the underlying software which enables the database to function. Some of the basic capabilities may be provided through the native data management portion of the operating system, upon which the database software is built. The rest is provided by the database software itself. Data Management is needed to provide organization, access, and control of the data that is stored on a computer system.

Besides being a necessary component of a database, database management provides benefits by providing and maintaining

structures, enabling data actions and enforcing data rules. It is substantially more productive for a given computer to perform functions with the database rather than to code the same functions in every program that uses the database.
Data Organization

Data organization facilities in a database must provide for a flexible data structure which meets today's application needs, yet can adapt to changing business requirements. Additionally, a database should be able to handle ad hoc requests for information as a by-product.

Data Access

Data access facilities in a database determine how you get at the data. They provide the ability to retrieve data, format data, and sequence data. It is through this software that the database is able to provide its data services to other constituent parts of the computer system as well as to user programs.

Data Control

Data control facilities in a database are also very important. They provide data independence from programs and assure the maintenance of data integrity such that, among other things, all database fields contain the correct data type
Life without a Database

Without a Data Base, there is no flexible data structure and data access is done by application programs. Security and control are provided by programmers through their individual programming efforts (very costly and time consuming, inconsistent, and not very secure). Additionally, without a database, many more programs need to be written.

For example, a new data selection needs new programs. Therefore, without a database, each reordering and each new selection increases the programming backlog. Another common example is a change to a file's record layout. Without database, input and output definitions must be hard coded in every program which needs to access the file. Thus, even a simple change to a record layout, such as a field addition or deletion, or even a change in a field length or an attribute means that each dependent program must be changed.

In summary, programs written without the help of a database, must do more work, and thus they contain more lines of code, are more expensive to build, are slower to develop, and are more difficult to maintain. Overall, they are not a long term good deal.

Types of DBMS Software

There are three popular types of database management systems (DBMS):

1. Hierarchical
2. Network
3. Relational

Hierarchical Database

Hierarchical databases create relationships in a hierarchical tree shape structure. Various files are linked together to form meaningful parent/child relationships using pointers that are imbedded in each database record. A customer record, for example, would have a disk pointer that would contain the order file address of the first order record for that customer. The first order record would point to the second; the second would point to the third, and so on. Programmers wanting to access the record chain would have to code for all of the navigation contingencies in their programs. Data access was not automatic.

Moreover, data queries were difficult to achieve, unless the database administrator had previously created a path which simplified the task. Ad hoc queries were very difficult to achieve.

Network DB

Network databases create relationships by maintaining imbedded pointers in separate join records. The relationships do not have to be hierarchical but, just as the hierarchical database, they must be predefined. Again, programmers must navigate through the database to achieve data access. Additionally, queries are difficult to achieve because of the pointer oriented data structure.

In many ways a Network Database looks like a hierarchical Database. You can certainly visualize it as a type of tree, though misshapen compared to a purely hierarchical structure. In fact, a Network Database, can be said to look more like several trees which share branches than one big tree.

Thus, in the Network structure, children can have multiple parents and parents can have multiple children. Despite this potential for confusion, because it addressed the inherent inflexibility of the purely hierarchical structure, it was looked on as a dramatic improvement, though far from perfect. One could not escape the reality that networking-based databases were difficult to implement and maintain. In fact, most successful implementations were of and for computer professionals, rather than real users. What was clearly needed was a simple model which could be used by real end users to solve real problems. From this came, the relational model.

Relational DB

The idea of a relational database was conceived and published by Ted Codd of IBM's Santa Theresa Labs in the ACM Journal in the 1970 time frame. His work was titled: A Relational Model of Data for Large Shared Data Banks.

Codd's idea was to create a database system, simple in concept, yet founded in sound mathematical principles. He knew with a proven mathematical theory as the basis for the database system, he could avoid the limitations, pitfalls, and anomalies inherent in hierarchical, networking, and other pointer oriented database implementations.

As an aside, while IBM was taking its time in the 1970's with its System "R" internal relational database project, a group of crafty technicians and entrepreneurs, led by Larry Ellison, who would later form a company which became Oracle Corporation, read Ted Codd's article defining relational database. They then set out expeditiously to build a software product based on Codd's theory.

The "to-be" Oracle company beat IBM to the punch, using IBM's original research work, and announced the first relational database software in 1978, a year or so before IBM was ready.

Relational database software has been a godsend to the industry. It combines the ease-of-use and ease-of-implementation characteristics of record oriented file systems with the structural and productivity features of existing database technology. There are no imbedded pointers. Files are brought together (joined) in structured views, external to the files themselves, based on relationships among the data elements (fields). Programmers need not know the implementation details in order to access the data. There is no complex navigation required for access.

For example, a customer record can be "joined" or linked to an order record using the respective customer number fields in both files. The files are "combined" when the join fields have an equal "relationship." The database software uses this relationship to create a virtual link between the two files. In essence, they are logically united. When accessed, the database presents a new "joined" record view of the projected fields in the files that is different from the record layouts of any of the based-on files.

Benefits of a Database Management System (DBMS)

Database management systems of all three varieties provide certain benefits to their users. The generic benefits of all database software are as follows:

- Data Sharing—Many simultaneous users of the same data
- Data Currency—Changes to data reflected immediately in all sequences
- Data Security—Data guarded by the DBMS
- Data Backup/Recovery—Facilities built into DBMS
- Programmer Productivity—Standardization of data definitions. Data base does record selection /ordering. Less duplicate work

Chapter 2. AS/400, IBM I & Relational Database

What's It All About?

AS/400 has an integrated relational database. A relational database consists of tables that are perceived to be stored in flat files or tables, regardless of their true underlying structure.

Unlike the complicated structures of the 1970's, records are linked by data, not by imbedded pointers. The database is conceptually easy to understand, thus making it usable by folks like us, who prefer to let the rocket science to the rocket scientists. With a relational database, for example if you have a set of data in physical structures, you can create new relationships simply by making a new table (view) and relating it to existing structures. The database supports all of the powerful data relationships, one to one, one to many, and many to many.

A relational file or table, called a physical file on the AS/400, is composed of rows, which are made up of columns. In relational database terminology, rows are called tuples; columns are called attributes; and tables are called relations. Tuples (records or rows) are logically linked together by the data in the attributes (fields or columns.) Each record in a relation (file, table) has a unique key which is called the primary key.

Renaming simple notions in IT for special purposes is not unique to the database realms. Long before database terminology, for example, there was file system terminology. In file system terminology, rows are called records, columns are called fields, and tables are called files. Now you know the big dark secrets of database and file terminology. However, it still may be a safe bet that you won't use the term "tuple" again in your AS/400 or IBM i career.

Database Operators

When Edgar F. "Ted" Codd devised his theory for a database structure founded in mathematical principles, his research was not intended for only the math inclined. In fact, Codd's wish was to hide the internal complexity from users while assuring logical simplicity and correctness within the database itself. He hoped to have a management facility and a language based on proven mathematical principals. In fact, Codd's wish was that users could access information from the tables he envisioned using simple English-like commands, as opposed to writing code. He found the following matrix algebraic operations quite helpful in building the data language which became SQL:

UNION
INTERSECTION
DIFFERENCE
DIVISION
PRODUCT
SELECT
PROJECT
JOIN

We find the most commonly used operations to be Union, Projection, Selection, and Join. These are supported on the AS/400 in SQL (DB language invented by CODD) and DDS (DB Language invented by IBM originally for the System/38.)

The other four operators are functions that are (1) somewhat more difficult to understand, (2) not as valuable, and (3) not supported by the AS/400 and IBM i. We will not cover these operators in this QuikCourse. If you would like a better appreciation of these algebraic relational operators, you may enjoy this Web article at:

http://www.codelearn.com/rdb/rdbd_rd1.html#operations

There is another relational operator which is very useful, but it is not listed as algebraic. The Order operation is most helpful in arranging data in sequences.

The Language which Ted CODD defined as the standard data manipulation language (DML) was called Structured Query Language or SQL. In this DML, Codd defined the operators, the structure, the syntax, and all the rules for manipulating a relational database.

Looking Closer at DB Operators

A more complete explanation of each of the five operators is as follows:

Order

As you can see in Figure F-1, ORDER sequences rows of a table without making a second copy

Figure F-1 Ordered and unordered records

```
    Unordered                        Ordered

|--------------------- |          |---------------------
|   Smith             |          |   Adams             |
|                     |          |                     |
|   Jones             |    ==    |   Brown             |
|                     |    ==    |                     |
|   Brown             | =========== |   Jones             |
|                     |    ==    |                     |
|   Adams             |    ==    |   Smith             |
|                     |          |                     |
|   Thompson          |          |   Thompson          |
|                     |          |                     |
*--------------------- |          *---------------------
```

Union

As you can see from Figure F-2, Union takes two similarly shaped files and creates one complete file from the two.

Figure F-2 Relational Union Operation

```
ORDER   MASTER1                              ORDER MASTER2
|-----------|--------|-------|        |-------- |-----------|-------|
|Order No   |Part No |Date   |        |Order No |Part No    |Date   |
|-----------|--------|-------|        |---------|-----------|-------|
|159244     |55511   |7/1/94 |        |187654   |34567      |4/21/94|
|           |        |       |        |         |           |       |
|263255     |29999   |7/7/94 |        |322456   |23456      |4/24/94|
|           |        |       |        |         |           |       |
|978121     |64444   |6/9/94 |        |457676   |44567      |4/30/94|
|           |        |       |        |         |           |       |
|. . .      |. . .   |. . .  |        |. . .    |. . .      |. . .  |
*-----------!--------!-------          *---------!-----------!-------
            V                                    V
            V                                    V
            V                                    V
                        UNIONED FILE
        |-----------|---------|-------------------|
        |Order No   |Part No  |Date               |
        |-----------□---------□-------------------|
        |159244     |55511    |7/1/94             |
        |187654     |34567    |4/21/94            |
        |263255     |29999    |7/7/94             |
        |322456     |23456    |4/24/94            |
        |978121     |64444    |6/9/94             |
        |457676     |44567    |4/30/94            |
        |. . .      |. . .    |. . .              |
        *-----------!---------!-------------------
```

Projection

Projection allows you to logically rearrange the columns in a table and also create subsets of the columns or fields in a table. As an example, in Figure F-3, you have a new view of the Payroll Master file, which does not include the salary. This view of the real data can be given to employees through relational projection. It is a projected image of a file which limits and/or rearranges the columns which are included in the view.

Figure F-3, Relational Projection Operation

```
   NAME     EXT      SALARY                  EXT      NAME
 |-------|-------|-------|              |-------|-------|
 |       |       |       |              |       |       |
 | Jones | 3677  | 16000 |              | 3677  | Jones |
 |       |       |       |              |       |       |
 | Smith | 3605  | 14000 |      ==      | 3605  | Smith |
 |       |       |       |      ==      |       |       |
 | Adams | 3939  | 17000 | ============ | 3939  | Adams |
 |       |       |       |      ==      |       |       |
 | Brown | 4200  | 35000 |      ==      | 4200  | Brown |
 |       |       |       |              |       |       |
 | ...   | ...   | ...   |              |       |       |
 |       |       |       |              |       |       |
 *-------!-------!-------               *-------!-------
```

Selection

Just as projection provides a subset of the columns in a table, selection provides a subset of the rows. If, for example, you wanted a view of all salaried employees who made more than $100,000 per year, more than likely, you would receive a subset of the payroll records . . . those which met that selection criterion. In the selection example in Figure F-4, (Just those customers from Michigan), you can see that the image after selection does not include A B Distributors.

Figure F-4 Relational Selection Operation

```
 |---------------------------|           |----------------------------|
 | ABC Inc      Detroit  MI  |           | ABC Inc      Detroit  MI  |
 |                           |    ==     |                            |
 | A B Distrib  Lima     OH  |    ==     | 123 Trucking  Alma     MI  |
 |                           | ========= |                            |
 | 123 Trucking Alma     MI  |    ==     | Allied Ent   Detroit  MI  |
 |                           |    ==     |                            |
 | Jones Inc    Akron    OH  |           *----------------------------
 |                           |
 | Allied Ent   Detroit  MI  |
 |                           |
 | Sun Ind      Tucson   AZ  |
 |                           |
 *---------------------------
```

In this process, the data base does the record selection. The program receives records which have been selected by the database. Since the database can fetch and test records substantially faster than a program, in addition to saving coding and the associated programmer time, using the database operators for selection also enhances performance.

Both projection and selection can be used for many purposes, including security. For example, a user could be authorized to a desired view of the payroll data instead of the entire file.

Join

With the JOIN operator, data in primary records (first file defined) gets joined with data from secondary records creating new "virtual" records with both sets of fields. Of course, more than two files can be joined. In fact, up to 32 files can be joined using the DB2/400 database.

To continue a join to a third file and to subsequent files, you would join the data in the 1st secondary file to that in the second secondary (tertiary – third) file. You would continue joining from file n to file n + 1 (where n = the sequence # of the last file joined and n + 1 = the sequence # of the next file to be joined.). You would be able to repeat this until you had no more joins to specify or you had reached thirty-one joins using thirty-two physical files.

There is no reason to include a particular file in a join logical view unless one or more fields from that file was going to be in the view provided by the file. We coined the term "virtual record" to describe the resulting record format after all of the files are joined and the fields from those files are picked and placed in the new record format of the new logical file. Thus, if a Join view consists of thirty-two files, it is safe to say that the record layout for that view contains at least thirty-two fields - a minimum of one from each of the joined files.

The JOIN operator plays upon the relationship of related fields - equal, greater than, or less than. In the example in Figure F-5, you can see that the Order Master file is joined (equal) with the Parts Master file so that the parts within an order can logically contain the parts description, which exists only in the Parts Master file.

Figure F-5 Relational Join Operation

```
ORDER  MASTER                           PARTS  MASTER
|-----------|--------|-------|          |--------|-------------|-----|
|Order No   |Part No |Date   |          |Part No |Description  |Loc  |
|-----------|--------|-------|          |--------□-------------□-----|
|159244     |55511   |7/1/88 |          |66342   |Size 7 Seal  |Whs 1|
|           |        |       |          |        |             |     |
|263255     |29999   |7/7/88 |          |18818   |No 12 ring   |Whs 3|
|           |        |       |          |        |             |     |
|978121     |64444   |6/9/88 |          |97676   |Brass plate  |Whs 1|
|           |        |       |          |        |             |     |
|. . .      |. . .   |. . .  |          |. . .   |. . .        |. . .|
*-----------!--------!-------            *--------!-------------!-----
         V                                      V
          V                                      V
           V                                      V
                         JOINED FILE
            |-----------|---------|------------------|
            |Order No   |Part No  |Description       |
            |-----------□---------□------------------|
            |159244     |55511    |CKK Valve         |
            |           |         |                  |
            |263255     |29999    |Left bracket      |
            |           |         |                  |
            |978121     |64444    |No 8 washer       |
            |           |         |                  |
            |. . .      |. . .    |. . .             |
            *-----------!---------!-------------------
```

As shown in Figure F-5, one or more data files can be joined together to create a view or "virtual image." The view is very powerful and presents a record image to a program or query as if all the data fields were gathered from one file. With such work being performed by the database itself, application programs can become much simpler to design and code.

Overall it is much easier for a programmer or for a Query user to work with a single, joined file instead of dealing with the complexity of multiple files. As previously noted, the AS/400 supports up to 32 physical files for a JOIN and the result is the formation of one new "joined" view of the data.

More on the AS/400 and IBM i Data Base

The AS/400 (IBM i) database is relational and has been since 1978. Not only did IBM select the relational model for the immediate predecessor of the AS/400 and IBM i machines, but the company also built the data base functions right into the heart of the machine.

Integrated Data Base

The System/38, in 1978 was the first computer ever built with a relational database integrated within the hardware and the framework of the system. The integrated relational database was and continues to be a hallmark of the AS/400 and the IBM i. There is no other machine in existence, even today, which comes with a built-in database. Can you imagine how far ahead of the competition the System/38 was in 1978 when DB2, IBM's mainframe relational database product had yet to be announced? And with a System/38, it was just there . . . and it was shipped with every box!

Relational databases by definition are flexible, natural, and simple to use. Yet there is a high level of sophistication in the capabilities and the low level implementation. Consider that one of the most frequently used operations in a relational database is index creation. The AS/400 has implemented this function as a hardware instruction. There is no argument that the AS/400 is a database machine since its inherent capabilities come from implementations that are not a part of add-on products but, in fact are built into the hardware and the internal code of the system.

AS/400 and IBM i Break DB Rules

Most relational databases use set theory and set oriented operations. Simple features such as the ability to link a compiler read and write operation to the database are not part of the deal. In fact, "compiler reads and writes to a database" are anathemas to the spirit of a relational database. Not only does it read and write naturally to the database, the compilers were written knowing the integrated database would be there.

The AS/400 breaks this big DB rule that data must be processed in a set. Not only does the AS/400 provide high-level SQL facilities and set operations with the data manipulation language, as you would expect any database to deliver, it also provides and in fact optimizes "natural read, write and update record-at-a-time oriented operations" to the database. You do not have to use SQL if you want to use an HLL compiler such as RPG or COBOL with your database. You don't have to define input and output for your RPG and COBOL programs because the compilers know about the database and copy the definitions in from the database at compiling time in much the same fashion as copy books.

Database Is a Given

In fact, the compiler writers, knowing that the very fabric of the AS/400 was its integrated database, used the natural APIs in the database so that normal HLL reads, writes, and updates to the database occur in the same way that other compilers access flat file systems. In other words, you get the power of the integrated database in program development built-in at the compiler level without having the pay the development burden of an add-on, unnatural facility that the compiler knows nothing about.

Moreover, the operating system provides major database recovery facilities that are just as built-in as the database. High performance journaling, and commitment control are built-ins – not afterthoughts, for advanced recovery scenarios. Many companies have used this support to deploy cross system journaling in which all of the updates on a given computer are mirrored via journaling on a computer in the next room or in the next city.

No Name Database -DB2/400?

In the early 1990's IBM did a survey of its AS/400 customers. It is a fact that many AS/400 customers have no or little professional staff keeping their systems running. The company asked AS/400 customers if the AS/400 had a database. Reportedly half of the AS/400 users did not know their machine had an integrated database. That's when IBM decided to use the IBM relational DB brand DB2 for the AS/400. IBM speakers often joked about this fact at conferences believing that their audiences would see the slam as a put-down to the less smart AS/400 programmers than the ones in the room! After all, they were not at the conference.

If It Has a Name, It Can't Be Integrated?

Of course that ruined one of my favorite pitch lines that I always felt put the AS/400 DB in perspective. Once I was able to say: "If it has a name, the machine knows nothing about it . . . If it has a name, it is not built-in, it is an add-on." Consider the plethora of databases which fit this mold: DB2 for all other platforms, Sybase, Informix, Oracle, etc. No compilers are aware of any of the hooks in these named databases. IBM wanted to make sure its customers knew that the company supplied a free database and a no-name version was not cutting it. Now, the AS/400 database has a name and it has the power of the best that IBM knows about a database. Corporate IBM's Santa Theresa Labs, where the relational database theory was invented, are now a big part of this new database for the future. And, it is still integrated with the machine.

To SQL or Not to SQL?

Despite its availability, and its acceptance as the industry standard, IBM chose not to use SQL as a native data manipulation language (DML), when the company introduced the AS/400 in 1988 and again when it introduced the IBM i in

2001. Instead the company used the same and only database model native to the System/38 – DDS.

DDS Was and Is Good!

That model was specifically built to help make it easier for IBM's small business computer customers to migrate to the System/38 platform and to use it without being burdened by even a modicum large system complexity. Changing compilers to use SQL and eliminating native "read and write" operations in favor of SQL were not in IBM's interests with either the AS/400 or IBM i announcements. However, the SQL data manipulation language should have become a standard system feature on a computer system whose claim to fame includes an integrated relational database.

It would not have been a good idea then, nor would it be a good idea now for IBM to eliminate DDS. Why would a programmer want to convert existing long-time-running code just to use SQL? They would not. IBM Rochester and Toronto, made the right decision to stay with what works - DDS!

The Official AS/400 and IBM i DML?

However, they purposely forgot to include SQL and should not have. Considering that IBM has been adding functions to the native database over the last few years which have just SQL support and no DDS support, it actually seems silly. How can an optional product be the gate for a native, integrated database? To not build the new function in DDS is also silly. We keep telling IBM to listen . . . maybe one day when we all start speaking to them.

Ask Big Blue this question: "What is the official AS/400 DML?" DDS is incomplete and SQL is optional. I guess there can't be an official DML for this integrated function. Sorry IBM. That is silly!

SQL is Optional

Shortly after the AS/400 was announced in 1988, IBM made SQL available as an optional database language for the system. In my opinion, the optional nature of the product was a mistake. It created SQL have's and have-nots for no better reason than IBM could account for its database revenue more accurately.

There was a runtime environment shipped with the operating system. Theoretically, with the runtime, package builders did not have to depend on SQL being purchased for their products to run. However, just like all COBOL package suppliers want COBOL on the user's machine, at a minimum for emergency fixes, so also do SQL developers want SQL on their users' machines.

It's Not in There!

SQL should have been built into the operating framework of the AS/400 so that all forms of database solutions could be maintained on every AS/400 - not just those machines whose users bought the SQL product. When Rochester IBM chose not to include SQL, the Lab added a "Mickey Mouse" characteristic to an otherwise elegant implementation.

From my perspective, the lack of integrated SQL has weakened, and continues to weaken the AS/400 and IBM i total development picture. Toronto fixed most of the other IBM i development anomalies in 2001 with the brilliant all-inclusive tool packaging of the WebSphere Development Studio for IBM i, 5722-WDS. With the Toronto Lab coming clean with application development in a big way as they have, either Rochester chooses not to see the light or Mother IBM is in control of the picture. Either of these scenarios is not good for the AS/400 and IBM i.

Chapter 3   AS/400 and IBM i Database Concepts

The AS/400 and IBM i Database

Now that we have made it through a few introductory chapters, let's take a closer look at what IBM built in 1978 as the native database.

AS/400 Basic Nomenclature

The mechanism IBM invented in 1978 for defining tables and views is still called data description specifications or simply, DDS. Relational tables and views built with DDS are implemented using what IBM calls physical and logical files. Physical files are regular old data files with data as you would expect them to be, though internally they have a few extra bells and whistles to accommodate record and field information as well s object information.

Logical Files are also called Logical Views, or just Views. A logical file is really just a view of one or more physical files. It has a similar object structure as a physical file but there is no physical data within the logical file object. It enables data access via a bunch of presentation rules which come into play when the logical file is used in a program or Query. These rules govern how the data in the "based-on" physical files, is to be presented when accessed via the logical view. Again, the logical file itself contains no data. Its access paths and / or indices point to data in up to 32 separate physical files.

That is our first set of specifics on the AS/400 relational database. No other relational database uses terms such as physical and logical files. Then again, since no other system has an integrated relational database, no other system could have compilers and utilities that are fully database-aware.

Are Physical and Logical Files Good?

A clever Windows implementer, wanting to win an argument – about which system is better, might suggest that, because no other system has physical and logical files, they must be bad. They must be a disadvantage to the AS/400 developer. This is far from the truth. In fact, because a database file - logical or physical presents itself to a compiler or a DFU utility or a Query utility as nothing more than a file, all of the database navigation is prearranged when you include a physical file or logical file in your program. You can do it all without a single Select statement.

Now, let us examine some more AS/400 specifics. First of all, in the integrated database, data items are stored in base tables. On the AS/400, again, these are known as physical files. Views of the data in the base tables are created using the relational operators which we have already discussed. The AS/400 native database calls these views logical files, and they are implemented using DDS specifications.

Of course, any database created with DDS (physical and logical files) is usable with SQL - both interactively and within high level language programs. The vice versa is also true. In other words, database tables and views created with SQL present the same file image to programs and utilities. Therefore, standard AS/400 programming (reads and writes) without SQL, can be used to access databases created with SQL.

Data Currency

The implementation of the database is done to accommodate data currency and immediacy. For example, any change to data is immediately reflected in all views. Moreover, there are no imbedded pointers or linkage records used to order the records, so there is not a big chain of events necessary when key data is updated or entered. All links are done based on the relationships of data, not by external, unnatural means.

Physical Files

Let's take a closer look at what makes up a physical file object on the machine. A physical file contains a definition of the fields in the file (a description of the data a.k.a. a format or database structure). It also contains an access path so the data can be stored either in arrival sequence (plus one access path) or in keyed sequence, such as customer number. The actual data in a physical file is contained in a sub-object called a member which is "contained" or "pointed to" from the file object.

Members

There can be many members in a physical file. Each member segregates a portion of the data from all other members. In normal database processing one member is accessed at a time. However, a file can be overridden to provide data from all members, one at a time. This helps in transaction-based systems. For example, it helps when data may be segregated by transaction date, and it helps at month end when the data is easily merged for reporting. Thus, we can envision that as part of every file, there is an "index" of members so that members can be accessed specifically by name. In AS/400 parlance, this is called a member list.

DDS Is Not Always Needed

Data description specifications (DDS) are typically used to create a native database. Using these forms, a developer can define a data record within a database. The record is known as a record format and it consists of all the fields which make up a physical record. Upon creation with DDS, a description of the format and the associated fields are stored within the database file object itself. Let's just say they are stored somewhere before record one of the data file.

Though this is the norm for formal database files, an AS/400 physical file can actually be created with no DDS at all. It is built with the "CREATE Physical File" command (CRTPF). The command permits a record length to be specified which structurally becomes the equivalent of one big field in the physical file database. Much like traditional programs using files, programs using such files would have to split the record into fields within the program. Logical files, however require DDS, since there is no other way using the Create Logical File (CRTLF) command to define the logical file selection criteria.

After data is defined to the database through source members, and the database is compiled with field names included, programs still do not have to bother with these descriptions. There is a switch for all high level languages (HLL) (column 19 in RPG/400 file description). The program says whether it will access data via records or use the field definitions.

To access the data into separate fields, programs can be written to (1) use the field descriptions in the database or (2) ignore the database descriptions and use input/output specifications within the program to distribute data from various "from" and "to" record locations into specific program fields. If option 1 is taken, HLL programs can also be written with no input and no output specifications, and the field names will actually be copied into the program from the database files at compilation time. That's what we mean when we say that the compilers and the utility programs are database aware.

Logical Files

AS/400 logical files are structured just like physical file objects and they behave in the same way as described above. But, they contain no data. Well, then what do they contain? They contain nothing more than a definition, or view, or set of rules as to how to retrieve records from a physical file or files and how to format fields when the file is used. Through the logical file, the AS/400 database is able to implement the relational operators, and send a view of the results of those operations to the requesting program.

A single logical file can be built over from one to 32 physical files. Any number of logical files can specify the same physical file as its source of data. Besides containing a possible, projected and/or selected view (field or record selection), a logical file is implemented with an access path. Therefore, just as a physical file, it has an efficient means of getting at the data in the physical file. The access path contains an index of key values and locations as to where the actual data record resides in the physical file. When a logical file is used, the logical file access path governs how data is presented or successfully retrieved from random operations.

Just as physical files can be used with either internally described data or externally described data, logical files work the same way. In fact, a logical file, with all fields defined can often be substituted in a program for its underlying physical file and the program would produce the same results as with the physical file. Of course, because data would be retrieved via a separate index, the program timings may be a bit slower.

Logical files are used to make new relationships in the data base from the existing database. As noted earlier, they support order, union, selection, projection, and join. Records can therefore be referenced, and/or selected based on data content, and/or subdivided (projected) based on data fields desired.

Data and Index Currency

Changes to an AS/400 database can be immediately reflected or can be deferred. When new records are added or when key values are updated in records, the access path must be maintained to reflect the changes. The system automatically updates the access path in all logical views either (1) immediately one at a time, (2) delayed, after the job is over, or (3) on a rebuild basis - the database rebuilds the index before every use. Based upon file usage, one of these approaches typically fits the database.

When you create your physical file or logical file or when you change the file object using either a Change Physical File (CHGPF) command or the Change Logical File command (CHGLF), you can specify your choice for access path maintenance. The parameter is used to govern all members of the file

The possible values are:

*IMMED   The access path is updated each time a record is changed, added, or deleted from a member. *IMMED must be specified for files that require unique keys.

*REBLD   The access path is completely rebuilt each time a file member is opened. The access path is maintained until the member is closed, then the access path is deleted. *REBLD cannot be specified for files that require unique keys.

*DLY   The maintenance of the access path is delayed until the logical file member is opened. Then the access path is changed only for records that have been added, deleted, or changed since the file was last opened. While the file is open,

all changes made to based-on file members are immediately reflected in the access paths of the opened file's own members, no matter what is specified for this parameter.

To prevent a long rebuilding time when the file is opened, *DLY should be specified only when the number of changes to the access path between successive open operations is small; that is, when the file is opened frequently or when the key fields in records for this access path change infrequently.

*DLY is not valid for access paths that require unique key values. If the number of changes between a close operation and the next open operation reaches approximately 10 percent of the access path size, the system stops saving changes and the access path is completely rebuilt the next time the file is opened. The access path is updated when the member is opened with records that have been added, deleted, or changed from the member since the last time the member was opened.

Chapter 4   Creating Physical and Logical Files

IDDU, SQL & DDS

How do you create physical and logical files? We have already briefly discussed two ways. There is a third method on the AS/400 and IBM i which was more or less imported from the System/36 to make migrations from that platform even easier. The three ways to create physical files are as follows:

IDDU   Interactive Data Definition Utility (used in S/36 environment)

SQL   Structured Query Language - optional

DDS   Data Description Specifications - AS/400 native interface to the database.

Interactive Data Definition Utility (IDDU)

Physical files can be described using IDDU. However, you will have to use DDS or SQL in order to build views of your data or to build logical files. You would choose to use IDDU if you are looking for a menu-driven, interactive method of describing data. You might also choose IDDU if you are already familiar with describing data using IDDU on a System/36.

In addition, unlike both SQL and DDS, IDDU allows you to describe multiple-format physical files which you can use with Query, Client Access, and DFU. Multiple physical record types are not supported via any relational database. All real physical database files have just one record format. These are created with SQL, DDS, and IDDU.

When IDDU creates a multiple record physical file, the database file itself remains unaware of multiple records since they are not supported. Query, Client access, and DFU, however, are application programs which can gain their record and field awareness by examining the IDDU dictionary in addition to the database information. These programs are written to support IDDU to make the migration to AS/400 from S/36 much easier than would otherwise be possible.

You can also use RPGII, RPG/400 or other HLL programs against these multi-format files but you must provide the record separation code as well as the input and output specifications within your program. The compilers are unaware of IDDU data definitions and get all of their database information from the database itself. When you use IDDU to describe your files, the file definition becomes part of the OS/400 data dictionary.

Because DDS has the most options for defining data for the programmer, this guide focuses on describing database files using DDS. If you would like to learn more about IDDU or you would like a better understanding of files, records, and files, IBM has a very nice book on its Web site titled IDDU use, # SC41-5704-00. It is very nicely done. Please check the Appendix in this book if you are unfamiliar as to how to find IBM's manuals.

SQL Structured Query Language

Of course SQL is the way everybody else does a relational database. Unfortunately, it is an optional, separately orderable, separately licensed program on AS/400. It uses the ANSI data definition, data manipulation, and data control language. SQL

is characterized by its simplicity and lack of verbosity. You tell
the system what you want. You do not tell the system how to
get it. One of the precepts of Ted Codd's relational design was
that the implementation details are unnecessary to the use of
the database.

SQL is certainly a fee-based alternative to DDS on the AS/400
and IBM i, but it has not had that much luck with old time
AS/400 programmers. It has been well-adopted by the newer
breed, who often come from other platforms such as Unix and
Windows. On every other platform, you either take relational
database the way Codd envisioned it, and that means SQL is
the standard . . . or you don't take the database.

The following is an example of a CREATE TABLE command
which is the equivalent of building and compiling DDS into a
database file.

```
CREATE TABLE  STUDENT
  (  STUDENT_NO  DECIMAL(10)   NOT NULL,
     STUD_NAME  CHAR(30)      NOT NULL,
     STUD_ADDR  CHAR(30)      NOT NULL)
```

This SQL command creates an arrival sequence physical file
named STUDENT with no key in the user's current library.

Data Description Specifications

DDS is the most frequently used method for describing the
database on the AS/400 and IBM i. The term data description
specifications actually defines DDS. There is one specification
form, which is identified by having an A in column 6. It is
known as the DDS form and it is used to describe data. The
form type of "A" differentiates it from all of IBM's other form-

based languages, such as RPG, which also uses column 6 as its form type designator.

At one time, database designers would actually use pencils and their DDS forms to design the database. They would then keypunch the forms or use the Source Entry Utility to get the specs into the system's source files. Now, designers use SEU directly and there is no longer a paper DDS trail. SEU is now used to directly create the record design or directly modify the record design within the source files. The pencil was voted out years ago.

The Six Levels of DDS

When you describe a database file using DDS, you provide information at one of seven levels:

1. **File**
2. **Record format**
3. **Join format**
4. **Field**
5. **Key**
6. **Select/omit levels**

Let's look at each of these levels in just a little more detail.

File level DDS gives the system information about the entire file. For example, you can specify whether all the key field values in the file must be unique.

Record format level DDS gives the system information about a specific record format in the file. For example, when you describe a logical file record format, you can specify the physical file that it is based on.

Join level DDS give the system information about physical files used in a join logical file. For example, you can specify how to join a number of physical files.

Field level DDS gives the system information about the individual fields which comprise a record format. For example, you can specify the name and attributes (length, data type etc.) of each field in the format.

Key field level DDS gives the system information about the key fields for the file. For example, you can specify which fields in the record format are to be used as key fields.

Select/omit field level DDS gives the system information about which records are to be returned to the program when processing (attempting to read) the file. Select/omit specifications apply to logical files only.

Creating Physical Files

Physical Files are defined to the system as fields comprising physical records of data and access to data. The definition of a physical file is file by name, record format by name, and fields by name and access by arrival sequence or keyed sequence.

IDDU Dictionary Support

Because of the existence of IDDU, I can no longer say there is no data dictionary on the AS/400 and IBM i. A data dictionary is supposed to naturally know about all files, records, and fields in the database system. Unfortunately, IDDU does not fit the bill. There is no data dictionary on the system. IBM had a shot at having one with IDDU but chose to make it a mimic of the IDDU on the System/36.

However, DB2/400 does come with reference database capability as a standard feature. Though this does not provide what the purists would call "active dictionary" support, it does permit system-wide or application-wide field dictionaries to be built.

Field Reference File - Data Dictionary

It happens that every normal physical data file on AS/400 and IBM i can also serve as a data dictionary. The term field reference file is typically used as the name for this function. The notion is implemented with nothing more than a standard physical file that contains database format definitions with field descriptions. By IT shop convention, the reference or dictionary file should not contain data. It certainly can contain data but the data layout would make no sense. The field reference file therefore is used as a reference for DB creation, as shown in the physical file compile diagram in Figure F-6.

Figure F-6 PF File Compile Diagram With Field Reference File

```
------------------,        ---------------------
|ARMAST            |        |                     |
|                  |        | FLDREFFILE          |
| ARMASTR          |        |---------------------|
|   R CUSTP        |        |                     |
|     CUST    R <...|.....|CUST     5N0  'CUST NO'|
|     NAME    R <...|.....|NAME    20A   'NAME'   |
|     STREET  R <...|.....|STREET  20A   'STREET' |
|     CITY    R <...|.....|CITY    20A   'CITY'   |
------------------         |... ---------------Physical Files
                           |...                  |
```

As you can see in the diagram in Figure F-6, at compile time, which is also known as physical file creation time, the DDS compiler visits the field reference file object to obtain the field attributes and descriptions. These "more complete" field definitions are built once in the dictionary and therefore do not have to be built in each specific file object.

In the diagram, on the left, you can see an inexact mockup of the DDS specifications as stored in a source file. More than likely, the name of the source file is IBM's convention – QDDSSRC. This incomplete DDS is in the process of being compiled.

On the right, you see another inexact mockup. This time it represents the field reference file. However, the field reference file as shown is not a source file. It has been compiled into a database object from its set of DDS which contained full attributes and descriptions. To the immediate right of each field name in the DDS (left side of Figure F-6), you can see an "R." This "R" tells the DDS compiler to use the field reference file to obtain the length, field type, column headings, text, and any other attributes that were coded for each field in the field reference file. Of course, as you would expect, if a particular field with an "R" code is not found in the "dictionary" (reference file), the DDS compiler will give an error message and not create the new physical database file.

The database implementation savings are obvious. You do not have to painstakingly define each field, such as customer number, in excruciating detail each time you want to create a database which uses the customer number field. Instead, you define it once correctly in the reference file. For each file that needs customer number, the "R" for reference code tells the compiler to copy the customer number attributes from the already-compiled reference object at object creation time. This saves saving lots of keying and it removes a major opportunity for error.

The CRTPF Command

When DDS is used to create any database file in a particular library, such as HELLO, a member is created at the same time. The member will actually "hold" the data when it arrives. Whether the DDS points to a reference file or not, the resulting file is built with a description of all the data elements (fields) – contained within the file object itself. To put this in perspective, any newly created physical file with its field definitions, can be used as the field reference file for another physical file creation. Moreover, this typically occurs long before any data is placed into the file

The CRTPF command to create a physical file is shown below with many of its default parameters. Following this command, we will briefly examine some of these parameters so that you can get a good feel about the information you must provide, and that which the system provides as defaults for the file creation process. Please note that this command will work regardless of whether the DDS uses a reference file or not. If a reference file is used, however, the file must be either available through the library list, or you must specify the reference library in the DDS. Otherwise, the compiler will not find the reference file. Now, let's take a closer look at the CRTPF command as follows:

```
CRTPF FILE(HELLO/ARMAST)
SRCFILE(HELLO/QDDSSRC)
SRCMBR(ARMAST) GENLVL(20)
FLAG(0) FILETYPE(*DATA) MBR(*FILE)
TEXT(*SRCMBRTXT)
MAXMBRS(1) MAINT(*IMMED)
FRCACCPTH(*NO) SIZE(10000 1000 3)
ALLOCATE(*NO) CONTIG(*NO)
UNIT(*ANY) FRCRATIO(*NONE)
WAITFILE(*IMMED) WAITRCD(60)
SHARE(*NO) DLTPCT(*NONE)
REUSEDLT(*NO) LVLCHK(*YES)
```

To better see all of the parameters involved in the CRTPF command with the English vs. keyword prompts, check out Figure F-6A below. If you were to hit CF11 with the panel in Figure F-6A displayed, you would see the keyword prompts as in the CRTPF command above.

There are two ways to get this prompt. You can type CRTPF at a command line and hit F4 for prompting or you can invoke PDM, select the DDS member to compile, place a 14 by it, and then you can hit F4 for prompting. The latter method will result in less keying since PDM supplies the name of the file object and the DDS information to the prompter.

Figure F-6A Create Physical File

```
                        Create Physical File (CRTPF)

Type choices, press Enter.

File . . . . . . . . . . . . . . > ARMAST        Name
  Library . . . . . . . . . . . >   HELLO        Name, *CURLIB
Source file . . . . . . . . . . > QDDSSRC        Name
  Library . . . . . . . . . . . >   HELLO        Name, *LIBL,
  *CURLIB
Source member . . . . . . . . . > LANGUAGE       Name, *FILE
Record length, if no DDS . . . .                 Number
Generation severity level  . . . > 20            0-30
Flagging severity level . . . . > 0             0-30
File type . . . . . . . . . . . > *DATA          *DATA, *SRC
Member, if desired . . . . . . . > *FILE         Name, *FILE, *NONE
Text 'description' . . . . . . . > *SRCMBRTXT


                        Additional Parameters

Maximum members . . . . . . . . > 1              Number, *NOMAX
Access path maintenance . . . . > *IMMED         *IMMED, *DLY,
  *REBLD
Force keyed access path . . . . > *NO            *NO, *YES
Member size:
  Initial number of records . . > 10000          1-2147483646, *NOMAX
  Increment number of records . > 1000           Number
  Maximum increments . . . . . . > 3             Number
Allocate storage . . . . . . . . > *NO           *NO, *YES
Contiguous storage . . . . . . . > *NO           *NO, *YES
Preferred storage unit . . . . . > *ANY          1-255, *ANY
Records to force a write . . . . > *NONE         Number, *NONE
Maximum file wait time . . . . . > *IMMED        Seconds, *IMMED,
  *CLS
Maximum record wait time . . . . > 60            Seconds,*NOMAX, *IMMED
Share open data path . . . . . . > *NO           *NO, *YES
Max % deleted records allowed . > *NONE          1-100, *NONE
Reuse deleted records . . . . . > *NO            *YES, *NO
Record format level check  . . . > *YES          *YES, *NO
```

Dissecting CRTPF Parameters

Now, let's dissect this command just a bit so we have a better understanding of what we are telling the compiler when we create a physical file.

```
File . . . . . . . . . . . > ARMAST
  Library . . . . . . . . >  HELLO
Source file . . . . . . . > QDDSSRC
  Library . . . . . . . . >  HELLO
Source member . . . . . . > ARLINQ
Record length, if no DDS . >
```

In the section above, you tell the compiler to create a file object
named ARMAST and that it should be built in the HELLO
library. You then tell it the DDS is in the QDDSSRC source
file which is in the HELLO library. In the second last line, you
tell the compiler that the specific DDS for this file is located in
the ARMAST member of the QDDSSRC source file. The last
line shows on the prompt but is not used. If no DDS were used
for the file, this is where you would specify the record length.

Generation severity level . . . > 20

This parameter specifies the severity level at which the create
operation fails. If errors occur that have a severity level greater
than or equal to this value, the command ends.

Flagging severity level . . . . > 0

This parameter specifies the minimum severity level of
messages to be listed.

File type . . . . > *DATA

This parameter specifies the file as a data file rather than a
source file

Member, if desired . . . . > *FILE

If you chose to use a set of DDS for your physical description
which was stored in a different member in the source file, you

would specify that member name here. In this case, we said use the same DDS member name as the file object to be created.

Text 'description' . . . . > *SRCMBRTXT

In this parameter you supply a text description for the new file object. The *SRCMBRTXT parameter is the default and it means that the text used to describe the source DDS should also be used to describe the file object.

Maximum members . . . . > 1

A member is a named, identifiable set of data within a file. Each file object can contain up to 32,767 members. However, almost all files, other than source files are built with a one member maximum. This better equates to the notion of a file on all other systems. In these, a file is just one set of data. The notion of multiple members in regular files (not source files) best plays when you want to segregate all data in a file by a specific transaction date.

As an example, let's say that you might have an invoice file with all data in one member of the file. You can create a separate member for the transactions representing each individual day of the week, month, or year if you choose. In many applications this has big-time value. Think of a file named Invoice and members named Monday, Tuesday, Wednesday, etc. When you see this, you've got the picture.

Access path maintenance . . . . > *IMMED

This parameter is fully explained in Chapter 3 under the heading Data and Index Currency.

Force keyed access path .... > *NO

In this parameter, you specify, for files with key fields, whether access path changes (index) are forced to disk along with the associated records in the file as governed by the FRCRATIO parameter described below. If you specify *YES, you minimize the possibility that an abnormal job end may cause damage to the access path that requires it to be rebuilt.

Member size:
   Initial number of records ..   > 10000
   Increment number of records .   > 1000
   Maximum increments ......   > 3
   Allocate storage ....   > *NO
   Contiguous storage ....   > *NO
   Preferred storage unit .....   > *ANY

The above parameters pertain to the size allocation and disk location for the file which is being created. The default file allocation is used. This says that there will be 10,000 records in the file and when it is full, it can be expanded with no messages or complaints up to three times for one thousand records each. When the file reaches 13,000 records, for subsequent file additions, the operator will be asked if it is Ok to expand further. Jobs do not bomb as on many other systems when a file has been outgrown.

The AS/400 file allocation routine is very smart and it quickly learns about the behavioral aspects of new files. It does not give 10,000 records initially. It gives a few hundred and then watches the growth rate to determine how much is given next. Thus, by definition, the system conserves disk space by not allocating all the storage for all the files unless it thinks it is needed.

Of course, you can override this with the fourth parameter above and tell the system to allocate all the storage at file creation time. This is rarely a good idea. Moreover, the same amount of storage gets allocated for each member so if you chose *NOMAX for the number of members, the system would try to allocate 32,767 times 13,000 records for this file. You would quickly run out of disk storage.

You may have certain instances in which you want all of the allocated storage to be contiguous on disk to avoid making the system fetch pieces of the file from all of the disk drives. This too is typically not a good idea since it interferes with the equitable distribution algorithms of the system. You may optimize one file while creating major sub-optimization on the system.

The last allocation parameter above, gives the opportunity to designate a specific disk drive, for a file. Again, this is generally not recommended because it interferes with the natural allocation algorithms and may cause more issues than any benefits which you may derive. The single level storage disk smoothing algorithms do a nice job of keeping your disk drives managed well. Taking on this burden yourself, would be mostly unproductive

Records to force a write . . . .   > *NONE
Maximum file wait time . . . . .   > *IMMED
Maximum record wait time . . . . > 60
Share open data path . . . . . .   > *NO
Record format level check . . .   > *YES

The five parameters listed above are covered in detail in Chapter 5 so we will defer that discussion until then. These attributes can be specified on the CRTPF command, the CHGPF command or the OVRDBF command as you will see in Chapter 5.

Max % deleted records allowed .   > *NONE
Reuse deleted records . . . . .   > *NO

These last two parameters let you specify some rules for deleted records. The AS/400 and IBM i database has the notion of hard delete. When you delete a record from the database, it is gone. However, by default, its former living quarters continue to exist. Over time, if your applications perform hard deletes, there will be more and more space in your file being occupied by the entrails of these formerly live data records. These two parameters help understand and manage this space.

You can specify the maximum percentage of file size that you will permit to have deleted records. You may set that to 10%, for example. At the time you reach 10% deletes, the system will complain to you and you can then use the reorganize physical file (RGZPFM) command in the off-hours to strip out the deleted spaces.

The percentage check is actually made when the member is closed so as to not create an error condition for any running jobs. If the percentage of deleted records is greater than the value specified on this parameter, a message is sent to the system history log (QHST) to inform the user.

You can also choose to reuse deleted records and fill them up with newly added records. Unfortunately, there are two caveats with this approach which may affect your ability to use this nice capability. These are:

1.   If *YES is specified on this parameter, the key ordering attribute for the physical file in the Data Description Specifications (DDS) source cannot be "FIFO" or "LIFO." The FIFO and LIFO DDS keywords will be covered in the DDS examples later in this QuikCourse.

2.   If a *YES value is specified for this parameter, the arrival order becomes meaningless for a file that reuses deleted record space. Records might not be added at the end of the file.

Though there are a few more parameters for the CRTPF which we could cover, they are somewhat obtuse, and require more knowledge than is appropriate at this time. For now, we'd recommend your taking the defaults for any parameters that are not clear to you.

Our friend, Mr. Logical file would get upset if we spent so much time and paper on helping you understand physical files if we did not take a nice stop over to the logical file station. Let's go there now.

Creating Logical Files

Logical files are defined to the system as a bunch of rules in much the same fashion as physical files. In addition to the create logical file parameters, the rules in logical file DDS cause record selection, projection, and other relational operations upon records from a physical file. In addition to the rules for access, the logical file also contains the means to accessing the data.

Defined with DDS

The definition of a logical file is provided in DDS in much the same fashion as a physical file. In other words, you specify file by name, record by name, and fields by name(optional). Fields are optional because if you choose to have all of the fields from the physical exist in the logical file, you don't specify any logical fields. If you specify any fields – that is all you get. When you specify fields in a logical file, you re performing relational projection since you are projecting a smaller image (of fields) of the physical file than actually Access in a logical file is provided in arrival sequence or keyed sequence . . . with or without select/omit criteria. You make the call. Figure F-7 shows the components involved in a logical file creation.

Figure F-7 LF Compile Diagram with PF and FieldREF

```
|------------------,            ----------|
|  ARLINQ DDS      |           |  HELLO LIB|
|                  |           |           |
|  * All Fields of |  >>>>>>>  |  The      |
.. ...|  ..ARMAST  |           |  Logical  |
|     |            |           |  File     |
|     |  * Key on CUST         |  Object   |
|     |  * Select/ Project|    |  ARLINQ   |
|        *-----#-----------|       ----------
|              |
|              |
/------------------,        /----------------|
|ARMAST            |       |                 |
|                  |       |  FLDREFFILE     |
|  ARMASTR         |       |-----------------|
|    R CUSTP       |       |                 |
|      CUST    R ...|.....>|                 |
|      NAME    R ...|.....>|                 |
|      STREET  R ...|.....>|                 |
|      CITY    R ...|.....>|                 |
-----#-----------  |       |-----------------|
Physical File              Physical File
With data records          With no data records
                           Reference purposes only
```

Collecting the Attributes

As you can see in the diagram, at compile time, which is also known as logical file creation time, the DDS compiler uses the physical file (ARMAST in this instance) to obtain the record and field attributes for use in the logical file build. The "dictionary" on the bottom right has no real role at logical file creation time. The diagram merely demonstrates that the physical file originally got its descriptions from the reference file. During the logical file compilation process as shown in Figure F-7, the logical file receives all of its information from the physical file ARMAST, upon which it is based.

Reference Notation from Physical File Object

On the bottom left you can see a mockup of what appears to be the physical file DDS as used to create the physical file object. The caption on the left, however, suggests this is not the case. It represents the physical file — not the DDS. Since this is just a mock-up, the box on the left is designated as the physical file. A logical file is based on the physical file, not the DDS which was used to build the physical file. The R's in the mockup are there to remind us that this file originally got its field definitions from a field reference file.

Inside this physical file object on the bottom left, but not shown in the picture, you would also find a record format consisting of a detailed description and the full attributes, of each of the fields. These would be listed just as they were originally provided by the field reference file. There is, in fact, a notation in each physical file field, which identifies the original reference file used to define a field. Moreover, if the field name happens to be different from the reference field, this information also reveals the specific field in the reference file which was used to provide the created field's attributes

The Logical Is Based on the Physical

Having said that – it should be clear that the logical file is not based on the field reference file. It is based on the physical file object, ARMAST. However, just as within the ARMAST physical file object, there is a designation within the logical file that a reference file named fieldref was used for field definitions. This information is propagated into ARLINQ and any other logical files that are based on ARMAST. Thus, the logical file object contains the same field reference information as the physical file itself. In a nutshell, if you use a reference file, it's like a bad penny. It won't go away too soon, and it seems to have a life of its own.

On the top of this three-box diagram, the third box, of course, is a mockup of the logical file DDS used to create the file object. The DDS would show any specified fields for projection, and any key fields for ordering, and any select/omit fields for selection.

Not shown is the indication of the name of the physical file(s) upon which this logical file will be built. Of course by the arrows in the mockup diagram, you know that the view is to be based solely on ARMAST.

In a full set of DDS for the logical file, the name of the physical file would be specified in the PFILE DDS keyword. Just as with a physical file, the DDS for the ARLINQ logical file is stored in a source file such as QDDSSRC in the HELLO library. On the top right of the diagram, you can also see that the object is being created in the HELLO library

This incomplete DDS, as shown, is depicted as in the process of file object creation. The output of the compilation process is the file object. The Create Logical File system command is implied but not shown in the figure. However, it is shown and dissected below. Its input is the logical file DDS in the top part of Figure F-7 (ARLINQ). Its output will be a logical file object on the right which will be built and stored in the HELLO library. AS/400 and IBM i Objects are always created from scratch using Create commands which always start with the letters C-R-T.

The CRTLF Command

Just as with a physical file, When DDS is used to create a logical file in a particular library, such as HELLO, a member is created at the same time. The member in the logical file does not "hold" the data as we can visualize in a physical file. However, the logical member does access its data by pointing to the member component in the based-on physical file.

Whether the based-on physical file used a reference file or not, the logical file is built with a description of all the requested data elements (fields) – contained within the file object itself. It gets it from the physical file. If no fields are specified in the logical file, DDS, all physical file fields in the record format are part of the logical file field descriptions. If a subset of the fields is included in the logical file DDS, then that subset is included in the logical file object. Unlike a physical file, however, no logical file, whether existing or newly created, can be used as a field reference file.

The CRTLF command to create a logical file is shown below with many of its default parameters. Following this command, we will briefly examine some of these parameters so that you can get a good feel about the information you must provide, and that which the system provides as defaults for the file creation process. Now, let's take a closer look at the CRTPF command as follows:

CRTLF FILE(HELLO/ARLINQ)
SRCFILE(HELLO/QDDSSRC) SRCMBR(ARLINQ)
GENLVL(20) FLAG(0) FILETYPE(*DATA) MBR(*FILE)
MAXMBRS(1) MAINT(*IMMED) FRCACCPTH(*NO)
UNIT(*ANY) WAITFILE(*IMMED) WAITRCD(60)
SHARE(*NO) LVLCHK(*YES)

To better see all of the parameters involved in the CRTLF command with the English vs. keyword prompts, check out Figure F-7A below. If you were to hit CF11, with the panel in Figure F-7A displayed, you would see the keyword prompts as in the CRTLF command above.

There are two ways to get this prompt. You can type CRTLF at a command line and hit F4 for prompting or you can invoke PDM, select the DDS member to compile, place a 14 by it, and then you can hit F4 for prompting. The latter method will result in less keying since PDM supplies the name of the file object and the DDS information to the prompter.

Figure F-7A Create Logical File

```
                        Create Logical File (CRTLF)

Type choices, press Enter.

File . . . . . . . . . . . . . > ARLINQ        Name
  Library . . . . . . . . . . > HELLO          Name, *CURLIB
Source file . . . . . . . . . > QDDSSRC        Name
  Library . . . . . . . . . . > HELLO          Name, *LIBL,
*CURLIB
Source member . . . . . . . . > ARLINQ        Name, *FILE
Generation severity level  . . > 20            0-30
Flagging severity level  . . . > 0             0-30
File type . . . . . . . . . . > *DATA          *DATA, *SRC
Member, if desired . . . . . . > *FILE         Name, *FILE, *NONE
Physical file data members:
  Physical file . . . . . . .   *ALL           Name, *ALL
    Library . . . . . . . . .                  Name, *CURRENT
  Members . . . . . . . . . .                  Name, *NONE
                + for more values
                + for more values
  Text 'description' . . . . . . > *SRCMBRTXT


                      Additional Parameters

Maximum members . . . . . . . . > 1            Number, *NOMAX
Access path maintenance . . . . > *IMMED       *IMMED, *DLY,
*REBLD
Force keyed access path . . . . > *NO          *NO, *YES
Preferred storage unit . . . . . > *ANY        1-255, *ANY
Records to force a write . . . . > *NONE       Number, *NONE
Maximum file wait time . . . . . > *IMMED      Seconds, *IMMED, *CLS
Maximum record wait time . . . . > 60          Seconds, *NOMAX, *IMMED
Share open data path . . . . . . > *NO         *NO, *YES
Record format level check . . . > *YES         *YES, *NO


                                                        Bottom
F3=Exit    F4=Prompt   F5=Refresh   F10=Additional parameters
F12=Cancel F13=How to use this display        F24=More keys
```

Dissecting CRTLF Parameters

Now, let's dissect this command just a bit so we have a better understanding of what we are telling the compiler when we create a physical file.

File . . . . > ARLINQ
Library . . . . > HELLO
Source file . . . .> QDDSSRC
Library . . . .> HELLO
Source member . . . > ARLINQ

In this section above, you tell the compiler to create a logical file object named ARLINQ and that it should be built in the HELLO library. You then tell it the DDS is in the QDDSSRC source file which is in the HELLO library. In the second last line, you tell the compiler that the specific DDS for this file are located in the ARLINQ member of the QDDSSRC source file.

Generation severity level . . . > 20

This parameter specifies the severity level at which the create operation fails. If errors occur that have a severity level greater than or equal to this value, the command ends.

Flagging severity level . . . . > 0

This parameter specifies the minimum severity level of messages to be listed.

File type . . . . > *DATA

This parameter specifies the file as a data file rather than a source file

Member, if desired . . . . > *FILE

You must choose DDS for your logical file description, unlike a physical file which can be built with no DDS. If your source is stored in a different member in the source file, than ARLINQ, the file object, you would specify that member name here. In this case, we said use the same DDS member name as the file object to be created.

Physical file data members:
Physical file . . . . *ALL
  Library . . . .
  Members . . . .
    + for more values
    + for more values

This set of parameters specifies the names of the physical files
and members that contain the data associated with the logical
file member being added by this command. A logical file
member can be based on all of the physical files and members
on which the logical file itself is based, specified by
DTAMBRS(*ALL), or the member can be based on a subset of
the total files and members, specified by:

Most logical files do not need anything specified here. This
needs to be specified only if your logical file is being built over a
physical with multiple members. Since most physical files are
one member files, the file information can be specified in the
PFILE keyword in DDS. We will cover logical file DDS later
in this book.

Text 'description' . . . . > *SRCMBRTXT

In this parameter you supply a text description for the new
logical file object. The *SRCMBRTXT parameter is the default
and it means that the text used to describe the source DDS
should also be used to describe the file object.

Maximum members . . . . > 1

A member is a named, identifiable set of data within a file.
Each logical file object can contain up to 32,767 members.
However, almost all logical files, are built with 1 member
maximums to be in synch with the underlying physical file(s).
Just as with a physical file, one member logicals better equate
to the notion of a file on all other systems in which a file is just
one set of data.

Access path maintenance . . . . > *IMMED

This parameter is fully explained in Chapter 3 under the heading Data and Index Currency.

Force keyed access path . . . . > *NO

In this parameter, you specify, for files with key fields, whether access path changes (index) are forced to disk along with the associated records in the file as governed by the FRCRATIO parameter described below. If you specify *YES, you minimize the possibility that an abnormal job end may cause damage to the access path that requires it to be rebuilt.

Preferred storage unit . . . . . > *ANY

The above parameter pertains to a particular storage unit to onto which to load the logical file. This permits you to designate a specific disk drive for the file. Just as with a physical file, this is generally not recommended because it interferes with the natural allocation algorithms and may cause more management issues than any benefits that you may derive. The single level storage disk smoothing algorithms do a nice job of keeping your disk drives managed well. Taking on this burden yourself, would be mostly unproductive

Records to force a write . . . .   >   *NONE
Maximum file wait time . . . . .   >   *IMMED
Maximum record wait time . . . . > 60
Share open data path . . . . . .   >   *NO
Record format level check . . .   >   *YES

The five parameters listed above are covered in detail in Chapter 5 so we will defer that discussion until then. These attributes can be specified on the CRTLF command, the CHGLF command or the OVRDBF command as you will see in Chapter 5.

Though there are a few more parameters for the CRTLF command, which we could cover, they are somewhat obtuse, and require more knowledge than is appropriate at this time. For now, we'd recommend your taking the defaults for any parameters that are not clear to you.

Now, before we get into DDS and some "live" examples, let's look at some of the other characteristics of the AS/400 and IBM i database, DB2/400.

DB2/400 Database Characteristics

The AS/400 database accommodates data sharing by multiple users – concurrent access to physical files and/or logical files. The system maintains data integrity and provides data Independence.

What is Data Independence?

Data is defined to the database independently of programs and devices such as workstations. Each field is completely described through DDS to the database, and is not affected via input/output specifications or data divisions within programs.

This has major programming advantages including dramatically minimizing the impact of change and reducing redundancy & storage requirements. The fact that data is described externally to programs provides many advantages to programmers. These include:

1. **Simplicity in writing programs**
2. **Less program maintenance activity**
3. **Less redundant coding**
4. **Improved documentation**
5. **Consistent record / field names**
6. **Improved integrity**

Just as in the Hertz advertisement, it's time for a "not exactly." You can certainly make everything be "exactly" as described above or data independence. However, as discussed in the section in this chapter, DDS is Not Always Needed, you can also create database files without using DDS by using the CREATE PHYSICAL File (CRTPF) command and specifying a record length as below:

CRTPF FILE(HELLO/NODDS) RCDLEN(200)
TEXT('Physical File-- No DDS!')

When you "cheat" an AS/400 and IBM i physical file from having its field descriptions, you also eliminate most of the possibilities for data independence. I know of no other database that allows you to skip the part about giving the database knowledge of fields. Because the System/38, the father of AS/400, and grandfather of IBM i, was designed to replace systems with no database, the ability to bypass the database was as important to the creators as the ability to use the database. The phenomenon of having a "record" defined in a database with no fields was accommodated by pretending that the whole record was one big database field. In the early days it was given the name Program-Described Files, to distinguish it from the other, and more expected DB data methodology which was called Externally Described Files.

Program-Described Files

Program-described files are database files that do not have the data descriptions stored with the file. This means that some programs, such as Query/400, cannot use these files without a method of determining the format of the file. (IDDU can serve as a method for Query.) Application programs written in a "high-level" programming language, such as RPG or COBOL, can use program statements (input / output, or data division) to describe the files and data they use.

When the program chops up the data, these files are called program-described files. A database file and its data descriptions, as chopped up by programs, are known only to the programs in which the descriptions are contained. These descriptions cannot be used by any other program on the system. Each program that refers to a database file and elects to provide its own input and output statements must contain its own set of data descriptions.

Impact on Conversions

When I managed conversions of System/3's and System/34's and System36's to System/38 and AS/400, I tried to make the most of the database's capabilities, without interfering with the simplicity of the migration. I would create my own version of program-described files. Rather than use the create command with no DDS, I would build which matched the fields used for files in some of the major programs in the application software being migrated.

Technically, I had created externally described files but because none of the migrated programs were written to use the database, the programs were happy to continue to use their input / output or data division statements to manage the chopping of the records at execution time. However, because I had created internal data descriptions inside the file objects, new work, such as Query/40, DFU, and new program development, and DFU's, was optimized.

Logical File Fields

As you will learn when you study logical files, the remapping and reworking of field names can be most helpful in accommodating migrations. The more names for a field that are given in a logical database file, the more likely a program, using this file, with field names involved in calculations, will be able to have those field names found in the external database. This makes cutting over to external descriptions easier than it would be if the fields were not defined and/or lots of field names were not used to assure HLL compilations.

Limitations of Program Described Files

There are certain considerations which limit the overall usefulness of program-described files. These include:

- Query can not use a program described file as it fits this description. Query and similar programs can only work with a database file that has data descriptions either within the file (externally described), or if they are linked to a file definition in a data dictionary.
- High-level languages (such as RPG III) supporting externally described files can not easily support program-described files.
- Descriptions of program-described files are not saved when the files are saved.

Externally Described Files

Externally described files have their data descriptions stored with the file. This means that some applications, such as control language (CL) programs, RPG programs, COBOL programs, DFU's or queries, only have to name the file they want to use; the system finds the related data descriptions.

These are called externally described files because they are described outside of the application program. In contrast to program-described files, externally described files can be used by any application (query, document, CL program) that accepts data described as a natural database object with field descriptions. Files crafted from DDS, SQL or IDDU descriptions are typically externally described. Exceptions are the no-DDS CRTPF option and the multi-format IDDU created physical file.

Chapter 5   Data Management Attributes

Defining Behavioral Rules

There are a number of unique data base characteristics which are contained as attributes of a physical file. In essence they define the rules of behavior for the DB file. One might call these data management rules, since they are implementation oriented, not definition oriented. In other words, Ted Codd would not care about them because they are implementation details and are not part of relational theory.

Despite the efforts of the great master Ted Codd, who's database ideal was for developers and users to have no concern for the underlying system implementation and attributes of any computer system deploying a relational database, the fact is that every database runs on a computer with its own personality. When you deploy your database on any type of hardware, or operating system, you will find some different knobs to turn.

There will be some different bells to ring. And, there will be some different whistles to blow in order for you to get everything the way you want – and still have a fine performing machine. It is simply unavoidable, though you can, in most cases ignore the underlying AS/400 and IBM i system and just take the defaults.

Most of the file attributes we are about to examine are originally placed in the file as a result of the Create Physical File command – CRTPF command. After the physical file is created, most of these attributes can be changed permanently by the Change Physical File Command – CHGPF. Changes to the file made with this command are permanent until changed again.

A smaller number of attributes can also be changed temporarily during execution using the Override with Database File command - OVRDBF. There are also some attributes which are invisible in the object but affect the file object only during execution. These attributes are given in the form of overrides with the OVRDBD command.

Database attributes most often pertain to your physical database files, although some attributes such as index characteristics / maintenance are part of a logical file. The number of attributes in the file object is always the same, however, regardless of how the file is built - SQL, IDDU, or DDS.

Let's start taking a look at these very powerful attributes, one at a time. It helps to remember that these database attributes collectively form the rules for a database file, and are in fact stored within the object itself.

Records to Force a Write (FRCRATIO)

The AS/400 and IBM i are boxes which use the notion of Single Level Storage. Inherent in this implementation is the concept that virtual memory and virtual disk are one and the same and present the image of a single level storage to the system. Everything therefore is addressed with its single level storage address and ultimately resolved to real memory or disk. Neither the user nor the implementer controls what may be in memory and what may not be in memory at any given moment.

Virtual Programs and Data

By default, on your AS/400 or IBM i, both programs and data are virtualized. Long after a program thinks that it has updated or written a new disk record, depending on system and file characteristics, the record may still be hanging around in memory. To developers who have chosen to implement without journaling, commitment control, and perhaps without RAID5 disks, the idea that an order record, as an example, may not actually be "really" updated on disk, causes some level of consternation. And it should!

If the system were to crash . . . Yes, the probability is low that the disk will crash tomorrow; however, it is very high that one or more disks will crash during the life of your system. If you use RAID5 or mirroring, you are in reasonably good shape for preserving records that have been written.

But, what about those records that have not yet been written to disk? Well, without journaling, you may not get the more recently written records back. If the system powers off without a UPS available for you to do an orderly shutdown, unjournaled records in memory disappear with the rest of memory's contents as soon as the system is deprived of power. If your journals are on disk drives that are managed independently of your main disk storage pool, (separate auxiliary storage pool - ASP) you can get your data back up to date as well as withstand a disk crash.

This course does not teach you sophisticated techniques such as commitment control and journaling, nor does it deal with other implementation topics such as RAID Disk protection, or auxiliary storage pools (ASPs). Most non AS/400 relational databases use journaling and commitment control because, quite frankly, their systems do not have the same reliability as an AS/400 or IBM i. Please note that it is best, even with AS/400 and IBM i to use journaling and commitment control in your applications. Regardless of how your system is set up, however, you need to be familiar with the Records to Force a Write (FRCRATIO) attribute of the physical file.

Protecting Data

This attribute determines the number of insert, delete, or update operations that can occur on records before those records are forced into auxiliary (permanent) storage. If the physical file is being journaled, IBM suggests a very large number or the use of the value *NONE. There is a caveat with *NONE in that it may cause long synchronization of the journal and physical files. More detailed IBM information on this topic is available in the CL Reference information in the AS/400 Information Center. You can use the Appendix in this book to help you find the right information on IBM's site. Additional information on journal management for your system implementer is available in IBM's Backup and Recovery book, SC41-5304. All of this information is available to you on IBM's web site.

The value *NONE is the default. If you specify nothing or if you specify *NONE with the CRTPF, CHGPF, or OVRDBF commands, there is no force write ratios. The system determines when the updated or added records are written to auxiliary storage, based on the activity of the system at a given time. In essence the AS/400 and IBM i use volatile memory as a cache mechanism as other systems use expensive cache memory. Thus, the AS/400 and IBM i gain in performance when *NONE or a large number is specified for the force write ratio. Unless you are protected by journaling, however, it is risky business.

You can also specify a number for the number-of-write-operations- before-force parameter. When you specify a number, you are telling the system the number of record updates or adds to collect before it forces them to disk. If you have no journal and no other means of protection, especially for a transaction file such as order entry, you get some measure of protection against a sudden power problem or system shut down by making the force write ratio equal to one record.

Maximum File Wait Time (WAITFILE)

Since the AS/400 is an object-oriented system, there is code within the object itself to give information about the object, even when the object otherwise cannot be used. One such attribute which delivers a response to a program is the WAITFILE parameter. This attribute determines the number of seconds that a requesting program will wait for the file resources to be allocated when the program attempts to open the file.

The file is aware at open time that the program is attempting to acquire it as a resource. If the file resources cannot be allocated in the specified wait time, the file object sends an error message to the program, in order to inform it that the wait time is up and the program is not going to get the resource. The program can either go away or attempt to open the file again. It can also be written to send an error message to the system operator complaining that the file is locked by another process, perhaps suggesting in the message that the operator quiesce the process in conflict.

This attribute has major value when resources are being unnecessarily locked, for it helps the system programmer determine how resources need to be allocated. On most other systems, when a resource cannot be obtained the program crashes or waits until the resource is available. Neither of these alternatives is typically desirable.

Possible Values

The possible values for this parameter have an impact on operations. If *IMMED is specified, for example, the requesting program does not wait. When the file is opened, an immediate allocation of the file resources is attempted. If it fails, the program gets the message

If *CLS is the value, the default wait time specified in the class description is used as the wait time for the allocation of the file resources. More information about the class object can be gained from system help text by doing a DSPCLS (classname - such as QINTER), and then pressing F1 or the HELP key. You can also search IBM's work management guide or you can use the IBM i Pocket Developers Guide which offers a detailed section about the class parameter.

You can also specify the number-of-seconds to wait via the CRTPF, CHGPF or OVRDBF commands. This value provides the number of seconds that the program waits for the allocation of the file resources. The valid values range from one through 32767 seconds, and the value is specified in seconds. If you have a job, for example, which is bombing after getting knocked off at night, because it cannot get a required file, while you are trying to fix the problem correctly, you can set this parameter to 32767. This gives the program about nine hours to acquire the resource and is most often preferable to bombing in the middle of a batch update run. More than likely the resource will free in this time period. Meanwhile you will not be as "under the gun" to find the real culprit and to solve the problem properly.

Maximum Record Wait Time (WAITRCD)

There is another WAIT attribute which is also very helpful in finding problems and in terms of providing work-arounds while the problems are being investigated. This attribute has to do with how long a file will wait, after being requested by a program to fetch a record before it gives up and sends an error message. This is what will happen if the record is locked by another process.

Wait, Don't Crash!

This parameter permits you to specify the number of seconds that any program is going to wait for a record to be updated or deleted, or for a record read in the commitment control environment with LCKLVL(*ALL) specified. If the record is not allocated in the specified wait time, the file complains by sending an error message to the program.

If you are setting this parameter with an OVRDBF, it overrides the record wait time specified in the database file, specified in the program, and in any previously issued OVRDBF commands. If you have remote files, such as DDM files (distributed data management) which access databases on other systems, the minimum delay time for these is 60 seconds so this value may need to be longer than the wait you would specify for local database files.

Wait Record Values

If you choose the *NOMAX parameter, the program waits indefinitely for a record lock. This is lots more than nine hours so be careful with this. If you specify *IMMED, the program does not wait at all. The file attempts to get an immediate lock of the record when the record is read. If it cannot get the lock, it complains by sending the program an error message.

Of course, you can also specify some number-of-seconds. The value provides the number of seconds that the program waits for the record lock. It gets you all the way from one through 32767 seconds (about 9 hrs.)

Records Retrieved at Once (NBRRCDS)

In this land of web programming and client server code, we sometimes forget about all of the batch processes which are designed and must be designed into systems. Along with batch processes comes sequential processing. Along with sequential processing comes the AS/400 and IBM i sort program as invoked via the Format Data command (FMTDTA). Yes, even with an integrated database, there is ample need to sort records into a particular sequence before running a program

OVRDBF NBRRCDS

The Records Retrieved at Once (NBRRCDS) attribute is not specified in the file itself and thus cannot be changed. It is invoked only via the OVRDBF and lasts until the job has ended or the override is deleted.

It does pertain mostly to batch and sequential operations, but NBRRCDS is not limited to sequential operations. With this value, you define the number of records the system will read from auxiliary storage as a unit, for both random reads and sequential reads, and will write to main storage as a unit. The amount of data actually read is equal to the number of records times the physical record length, not the logical record length. Since the valid values range from one through 32767, as you can see, this parameter has the ability to affect performance in a very positive or very negative way.

It is valid for both sequential and random processing and should be specified only when the data records, which are fetched as a block, are physically located on disk in the sequence in which they are typically processed. If you guess wrong on this parameter, such as specifying a large number of records, say a thousand, with random processing, for a file that is not well sequenced, each random physical disk read will bring in 1000 records, though only one record in the block is needed for processing. That's a lot of wasted power.

On the other hand, if you are randomly processing (RPG CHAIN for example) by relative record number in record sequence, you will save 999 physical reads by setting this parameter as 1000. The first time your program requests records, a physical read is performed of 1000 records – in one fell swoop. If the next read your program makes (logical read) within the block is satisfied, no physical disk I/O is performed. If all 1000 records are retrieved within the block then the one physical block read accounts for 1000 logical record reads. When the program requests record 1001, the next physical block is retrieved.

As a final caveat with this approach, you must consider how much memory you have available. If, for example, you lug 1000 big records into memory, and the system needs this space for programs or other, higher priority data, your block will be paged out, and the system will fault and, your data will have yo be retrieved from the page data set on disk when the program does its next logical read.

EOF Retry Delay in Sec (EOFDLY)

Another processing setting carried by the file object and triggered only by an OVRDBF command, is the EOF – end-of-file – retry delay in seconds or (EOFDLY) attribute. With this parameter, you specify the number of seconds of delay before the system will try to read additional records when an end of file condition is reached in a program reading the overridden file. The typical happening for a program when it fetches a record after the end of file is reached is that the request is denied. No more records can be read from the file until the program either closes and reopens the file, or the program ends and restarts. In both of these cases, however, in order to get to newly added records while processing sequentially, the program must read through all of the beginning records, one at a time, and it must have information about where the new records begin.

No EOF Message

EOFDLY does not trigger the typical file close logic in programs. The file does not send an EOF message to the program. The program is disconnected from the file, and the program then sleeps for a period of time. The database physical file object wakes up periodically (1 second to 99999 seconds) as set by the EOFDLY parameter and it checks to see if there are more records to process. If there are more records, it starts shipping the newly retrieved records to the program for processing.

When you choose to use this technique, the delay time is used to allow other jobs in the system an opportunity to add records to the file, and have the new records processed without having to start the job again. When the delay time ends, the job is made active, and data management determines whether any new records were added. If no new records were added, the job waits for another time delay without informing the application program. When a number of seconds is given, no end of file occurs on the given database file until an End Job (ENDJOB) command or forced end of data (FEOD) occurs

How Does the Program End?

There are several ways to end a job that is waiting for records due to an EOFDLY wait. They are as follows:

- You can write a record to the specified file which is recognized by the application program as a last record. For example the key field can say END or be filled with Z's or 9's. The application program may then do a force end of data (FEOD) to start the end-of-file processing or close the file.

- You can end the job using the controlled value (ENDJOB OPTION(*CNTRLD)) with a delay time greater than the time specified on the EOFDLY time.

The DELAY parameter time specified would then allow for the EOFDLY time to run out, plus have enough time left to process any new records that may have been added to the file, as well as any end-of-file processing that is to be done in the program. The end-of-file is set by database, and a normal end-of-file condition occurs after new records are retrieved.

- You can end the job immediately (ENDJOB OPTION(*IMMED)). If the job is interactive, just start a system request and end the previous request.

If you choose *NONE as the value then it is like you have chosen not to use the EOFDLY. Normal end-of-file processing is done. If you specify a number-of-seconds, then the program waits that long between attempts to get a record when the file object senses an end of file condition. No end of file is signaled until force end of data occurs, or until the job is ended with the *CNTRLD option. Valid values range from 1 through 99999 seconds. That's about 30 hours at max.

Record Format Level Check (LVLCHK)

We've looked at performance attributes and program facility attributes and now we are going to look at an integrity attribute. The Record format level check (LVLCHK)attribute specifies whether the level identifiers for the record formats of the database file should be checked when the file is opened by a program. For this check, which is done while the member is opened, the system compares the record format identifiers of each record format used by the program with the corresponding identifiers in the database member. Level checking cannot be done unless the program contains the record format identifiers. You cannot use an override to change level checking from *NO to *YES, but you can turn it off with an override.

An Indelible Mark

When a database file is created (logical or physical), the compiler prints some identifying information within the created file object. A unique stream of data is associated with each of the different formats in the file during the process. It is known as "level information" or more formally as record format identifiers.

When a program is compiled that uses a database file, the compiler copies this unique "level information" into the created program object. In this way, the program "knows" the shape of the file as it was on the day the program was compiled. The object program is built to accommodate that shape. If you go ahead and change that database file, the system will reward you by building a new set of "level information" into the file object. This will make your program bomb. It will bomb with a level check error at file open time, since the file signature is not the same as when the program was compiled. If the program is based on one shape of data and you change the shape, you want the program to bomb before it messes something up. This is exactly what happens. It serves to protect program and database integrity.

How Do You Get the Levels in Synch?

So, this is good overall. But it may be bad temporarily. Let's say, for argument purposes, that you added a field to the end of a record and you recreated the database. Let's also say that the program you are working with, does not need the additional field or fields you added. If you do nothing extra, your program will bomb. However, if you compile the database with LVLCHK(*NO) or you override it at execution time, you can avoid the costly level check and your program will run fine.

The down side is that you will have degraded the value of the level mechanism and you will have lost a valuable means of protecting program and database integrity. The right thing to do, for integrity purposes, after a major database change, is to recompile all affected programs. This recaptures the level information and gives the compiler the opportunity to assure that all is OK before building the new program object. Share Open Data Path—ODP (SHARE) Now, we come to an attribute that helps us control file sharing. Again, not exactly! The Share Open Data Path (SHARE) attribute determines whether the open data path (ODP) is shared with other programs in the same routing step. When an ODP is shared, the programs accessing the file share facilities such as the file status information and the data buffer.

What is an ODP?

You can think of an ODP as the information in a job about a file. For example, one of the things a job knows about a file it is processing is the address of the current record, and, if processing is consecutive, it knows which record will be processed next. When an ODP is shared, more than one program in a job stream is aware of the processing information such as the file cursor (the "which record" pointer).

Suppose program A opens up a file with a shared ODP. Let's say it then reads two records and calls program B. Program B in turn, opens the same file with a shared ODP. When program B reads the file, it is presented with record 3 of the file, not record 1, since it has elected to share the open data path with program A.

There are a few choices when specifying whether you want the ODP shared or not. If the value is *NO, then the ODP is not shared with other programs in the routing step (job). A new ODP for the file is both created and used every time a program opens the file. On the other hand, if you select *YES for the attribute, the same ODP is shared with each program in the job.

Limit to Sequential Only (SEQONLY)

The Limit to Sequential Only (SEQONLY) is another processing-only attribute. It has some similarities to the number of records (NBRRCDS) parameter discussed above, but it is not the same. In fact, it takes over after the NBRRCDS parameter finishes doing its thing. Moreover, as you will soon see, the SEQONLY parameter has its own number of records sub-parameter. Its job, when specified in the OVRDBF command is to stage the physical file for sequential - only processing. In other words, it specifies, for database files whose records are processed in sequential order only, whether sequential only processing should be used with this file. It will help avoid confusion if I show you how this thing looks in a prompted override (OVRDBF) as follows:

Limit to sequential only: **SEQONLY**
Sequential only ....   **> *YES**
  Number of records ......   **> 100**

From Disk to Virtual Memory and Back

This parameter also specifies the number of records transferred as a group to or from the database (virtual memory) if sequential only processing is used. If a number is not specified, a default number is handily determined by the system. You are better off specifying your own number. This parameter is used to improve the performance of programs that process database files in a sequential manner. It overrides any blocking value specified in the program or in any other previously issued OVRDBF commands.

The SEQONLY parameter also specifies the number of records (NBRRCDS) transferred from database pages (in virtual memory) to the application program's data management buffer. This is not the same as and is not to be confused with the

NBRRCDS parameter which we discussed earlier. This standalone NBRRCDS parameter has to do with how many records are fetched into virtual memory from the disk drives. The SEQONLY NBRRCDS parameter has to do with how many records are fetched at a time from virtual memory (may be real memory) and are placed into the data management buffer within the program.

When records are in virtual memory, they are visible to all applications, and in fact, can be updated by other applications as long as they are not locked exclusively. On the other hand, when records are in a program's buffer, they are only available to that program or other programs in that job is ODP sharing is enabled.

□ Hint: If you would like to study this topic even further, you can go to The "SEQONLY and NBRRCDS Parameters" topic in the "DB2 UDB for IBM i Database Programming V5R1" manual on IBM's web site. The specific entry at the time of this writing is as follows: http://publib.boulder.ibm.com/pubs/html/as400/v5r1 /ic2924/info/dbp/rbafomst193.htm#IDX3795.

If you are not on V5R1 or otherwise have a problem with this URL and you can't get there from here, feel free to use the Appendix in the back of this book to help you find this manual or any other IBM manual in the IBM Information Center.

Chapter 6   The Database File Object & DB Theory

DDS by Example

We are closing in on the "learn-by-example" part of the book. In the next few chapters, after we painstakingly analyze the file object and the DDS form, you will rapidly go through a number of very valuable and highly usable coding examples. First, however, we set the stage about DDS created databases. Next, we'll get you started coding simple physical database file DDS, then more complex, then simple logical files, then union and multi-format logical files, and then we take a big hit at join logical files. Before you know it, you will be on your way, to being a database guru.

□ Hint: We know that you have done a lot of reading up until now and there is more to go before we hit the examples. It is good to read all of these chapters before the examples so that you have a better appreciation for what is in the examples. We would also recommend reading this material again after you have studied the examples. We expect that you will find that this material can serve you both as a means of learning more about the IBM i and AS/400 database and a quick and handy database reference tool.

Let's first take a look at what might be inside a payroll earnings
master physical database file object. See Figure F-8.

Figure F-8 Earnings Physical File

```
Format
R   EARNMSTR                    LENGTH DEC
EMPNAM      25  0
EMPINL       2
ACCT#        6  0
PAYCOD       1
RATE         6  2
EMPNO        6  0
           . . .
Access Path
Key is EMPNO
Data

        Data
        Member 1

           Record1
           Record2
           Etc.

              Member 2
                 . . .
```

The Makeup of a File Object

As you can see in Figure F-8, a database file object consists of a
number of different parts. The three key elements of a database
file object are the record format, the access path and the data.

Record Format Information

The first part is the format information. In this section of the
database object, the system maintains the format name and the
field names. The sum total of all the fields is referred to as the
format. Though at first it does not seem necessary to have a
name for a database format, the more you study DDS for

physical, logical, display, and printer fields, the more the format name notion makes sense.

Physical File - One Format

Why not just use the file name as the format name? That would work for physical files since a physical file is permitted just one format. The data in a physical file can be shaped just one way. That is a precept in relational database theory. You cannot have two different record types in a physical file. If you need two different record types, then you must define the different record types as separate physical files since the rules for physical files say that you can only have one format. The rules also say that one format must have a name which is different from the name of the file.

Display & Printer Files - One or More Formats

Logical files, display files, and printer files are also built with DDS. All three of these file object types can have more than one format. For display files, a format is used for each display panel within the display file. For printer files, a format is used for each different shaped area of a report - report headings, column headings, detail lines, and totals.

Logical Files - One Format

When a simple logical file is built on one physical file, it consists of just one format. Logical files can also be built over multiple physical files. You may say: "Of course! After all, that is how you perform a join." However, just as a physical file or a simple logical file is limited to one format, so also is a join logical file. It has just one format. It is a new format, created within the logical file from fields which exist in formats from different physical files.

Though a join logical file can be built from one or many physical file formats, it does not preserve the named physical file formats within the logical file. Instead it rearranges the fields from all the formats into a unique shape for its own purposes. The result of the rearrangement is one new named join record format that consists of fields from the one or more physical files that are participating in the join logical file.

Logical Files - Multiple Formats

If simple logical files and join logical files consist of just one record format, how would a logical file ever use more than one physical file format? Good question! There is a type of non-join logical file which can be built over multiple physical files. It is called a multiple format logical file. Through the multiple-format logical view, the formats from multiple physical files can be included in tact and fully complete. However, if data re-arrangement or field sub-setting within one, any, or all record formats is needed, projected record views of the physical file formats can also be built.

This is a unique capability for the AS/400 database. No other relational database offers support for multiple formats in a data view. By constructing a multiple format logical view, the AS/400 can project a pointer-less hierarchical image of data, even though the real data is kept in simple relational tables (physical files)

In addition to providing a hierarchical view of data, this mechanism also enables systems designers to simulate the flat file notion of multiple record formats in a physical file. Let's look at a simple example of four physical files with each file consisting of a differently shaped record format.:

1. Customer Order File
2. Order Miscellaneous File
3. Order Detail File
4. Order Total File

If the AS/400 and IBM i were not using database files, of course all of these record types could be included in one physical file in there are no field definitions. As discussed in earlier chapters, such a file could be built with the CRTPF command by specifying a record length large enough for the largest record format. The file could also be created with IDDU so that it could be used in Query/400 reports. In both of these scenarios, however, any RPG or other HLL program which processed the file would have to describe the fields internally to the program.

If the four physical files were created, a multiple format logical file could be built on top of the four files. By using DDS to specify a key for each format, the system would create an index as if the files had been sorted by order number and order line number. In this way, the logically "sorted" order records would be presented to a processing program, such as a pick list program, one order at a time. The view would intermingle the records from the four files in the sequence specified above - customer order record, miscellaneous record, detail records, and the total record to produce pick lists, acknowledgments, registers, and invoices as if the order records were together in the same file.

☐ Hint: Good news. There is more descriptive information about multiple format logical files in Chapter 13 under the heading – Multiple Formats - One Set of DDS. Ther is also an example of how to code a multpile format logical file. Feel free to take a peak now, but please return so that you can assure yourself of the full value of this book.

The EARNMSTR Record Format

The peek we took of the EARNMAST file as shown in Figure F-8 was a simple physical file with no field reference file definitions shown. The format name in this file object is:

EARNMSTR

Since a format is not much more than a named record layout, the rest of the format as shown in Figure F-8 consists of the following fields and their associated lengths and attributes:

	LENGTH	DEC
EMPNAM	25	0
EMPINL	2	
ACCT#	6	0
PAYCOD	1	
RATE	6	2
STATUS	1	
EMPNO	6	0
MGRNO	6	0

Though we show only the length, type, and decimals in the above field list, fields can possess a number of attributes. Many of the attributes are defined in the database so that they can be used in programs. For example, a field can have an alias of up to 30 characters so that it can be used in an existing COBOL program in its full size. The record format named EARNMSTR also contains some text and some column headings as record and field attributes. You can see these in the DDS which was used to build the file object - Figure F-9.

Access Path

The access path is a vital part of every physical and logical file. Considering that physical and logical files are similar in their object organization, both have a component for access path. So, just what is an access path?

The simplest definition of an access path is as follows: An access path is a file object component that describes the order in which records are to be retrieved. Records in a physical or logical file can be retrieved using an arrival sequence access path or a keyed sequence access path. Logical files can get a little fancier. In addition to ordering records via the access path, they provide a means to perform record selection or omission. This permits you to select and omit records based on the value of one or more fields in each record. If a record is selected by the access path rules, it can be selected for processing.

Arrival Sequence Access Path
What is arrival sequence? Another great question! When a key field is not used to arrange the records of a particular type within a file member, an arrival sequence access path is used. This type of access path is based on the order in which the records arrive and are stored in the file. For reading or updating a data file object, records with an arrival access path can be accessed in two different ways:

✓ Sequentially—In sequential processing, each record is taken from the next sequential physical position in the file.

✓ Directly—In direct processing by relative record number, a record is identified by its position from the start of the file.

For the reader who is already coding this stuff in her or his head, an externally described file is given an arrival sequence access path when the database designer provides no key fields for the file.

Keyed Sequence Access Path

A keyed sequence access path is based on the contents of the key fields as defined in DDS. This type of access path is updated whenever records are added or deleted, or when records are updated and the contents of a key field, is changed.

> ☐ Hint: For more information as to how to manage when the access path gets updated, see Chapter 3 under the heading, Data and Index Currency.

The keyed sequence access path is valid for both physical and logical files. You define the sequence of the records in the file using the key level in DDS when the file is created. The access path sequence is maintained automatically by the system. As you would expect, the system creates an internal index by key which points to the relative record number of the associated data record.

Sharing Access Paths

AS/400 and IBM i data management is very efficient. If you create a logical file with a keyed access path, and a keyed access path or a super-set of the keyed access path that you want already exists on the file, OS/400 will point your access path to the access path which satisfies the rules you have provided without building a new index.

There is also a little tool which you can use yourself to assure that the attributes of a particular access path is used by the logical file you may be creating. You can use the DDS keyword REFACCPTH (reference access path) to use another file's access path specifications. When your file is created, the system always determines which access path to share. The file you are creating with the REFACCPTH keyword does not necessarily share the access path of the file specified in the REFACCPTH keyword. This would fool the greatest of assuming minds. Though I too had always assumed that the REFACCPTH file would be the path that my file would share, I eventually learned this was a false assumption.

The REFACCPTH keyword is used to simply reduce the number of DDS statements that must be specified. That is, rather than code the key field specifications for the file, you can specify the REFACCPTH keyword at the file level in your DDS (shown below). When the file is created, the system copies the key field and select/omit specifications from the file specified on the REFACCPTH keyword to the file being created.

Though we are not really working the examples en masse yet, it would help for you to see how this is specified in DDS.

```
00010A* EARNLMS2 Earnings Logical File
00020A                 REFACCPTH(HELLO/EARNLMS1)
00030A  R EARNMSTR    PFILE(EARNMAST)
```

Notice above that these DDS statements create a logical view against a physical file called EARNMAST (shown in statement 00030). The new logical file will have the name EARNLMS2 as shown in the comment statement in statement 00010. The REFACCPTH keyword tells the compiler to go into the logical file EARNLMS1 and copy any key level and select omit level attributes into the EARNLMS2 logical file which is being created, even though there are no DDS statements for the key field or the select omit fields in the sample shown above.

Processing by Relative Record Number
Through a program written in a high-level language (HLL), such as RPG, or via the Display Physical File Member (DSPPFM) command, or the Copy File (CPYF) command, you can process a keyed sequence file in arrival sequence. You

can use this function for a physical file, a simple logical file based on one physical file member, or a join logical file.

In essence though some files have only an arrival sequence access path, even keyed files have an arrival sequence access path, in addition to the keyed access path. It does not take up any additional storage and it is always saved or restored with the file.

☐ Hint: You may have already guessed the secret. The arrival sequence access path is nothing more than the physical order of the data as it was stored, when you save the data you save the arrival sequence access path.

The example shown in Figure F-8 shows that the EARNMAST physical file object has been built with a key, and the key is EMPNO.

Data

The ability to carry data comes to the physical file through the notion of members. It is actually the member in a database file (physical or logical) which point to the data components in a physical file. If the member is part of the physical file, the data component is part of the same file object. If the data is part of a physical file, and you are creating a logical file, the data sub-object in the logical file (the logical file member) points to the data in the based-on physical file(s).

Create a Physical File
The simplest way to have a data bearing file (physical) on the AS/400 is to use the Create Physical File command. This is the command we use below to build the EARNMAST file with the DDS as supplied in Figure F-9. The command to create EARNMAST would look very similar to the command shown below:

```
CRTPF
FILE(HELLO/EARNMAST)
SRCFILE(HELLO/QDDSSRC)
SRCMBR(EARNMAST)
GENLVL(20)
FLAG(0)
FILETYPE(*DATA)
MBR(*FILE)
TEXT(*SRCMBRTXT)
MAXMBRS(1)
```

☐ Hint: In Chapter 4, under the heading The CRTPF
Command, we provided a first look at a full Create
Physical File command. You may want to review this
information before proceeding.

The last three of the four above parameters tell the system that
this will be a data file – FILETYPE(*DATA), and it will have
1 member – MAXMBRS(1), and that member will be named
the same as the file name – MBR(*FILE).

Create a Logical File

To balance our coverage of the file types, the command to
create the EARNLMS2 file described above is as follows:

```
CRTLF
FILE(HELLO/EARNLMS2)
SRCFILE(HELLO/QDDSSRC)
SRCMBR(EARNLMS2)
GENLVL(20)
FLAG(0)
FILETYPE(*DATA)
MBR(*FILE)
DTAMBRS(*ALL)
MAXMBRS(1)
MAINT(*IMMED)
```

⬜ Hint: In Chapter 4, under the heading The CRTLF
Command, we provided a first look at a full Create
Logical File command. You may want to review this
information before proceeding.

You may be able to immediately observe the one major
parameter difference for the logical file. The last five
parameters above have a major role in the behavior of the
logical file. Just like in a CRTPF, these parameters tell the
system that this will be a data file – FILETYPE (*DATA), and
it will have one member – MAXMBRS(1), and that member
will be named the same as the file name – MBR(*FILE). These
are the same as when creating a physical file.

The third last parameter – DTAMBRS(*ALL) is unique to the
CRTPF command. It tells the system that this logical file is to
be based on all of the members of the referenced physical file.
Since there is only one member in the physical, the logical will
be created with just one member.

The next parameter – MAINT(*IMMED) is also available as a
parameter on the CRTPF command for keyed access physical
files. Because a logical file has no real data, the access path

maintenance parameter is always something which you should think about and decide, based on the application.

Members Provide Data Access

You cannot create a physical or logical file that does not point to at least one data bearing member. Of course when you create the physical file, the member contains no data but it has the ability to contain data. A logical file member never points to data in a logical file object since a logical file object has no room for data. However, a logical file member is structured very similarly to a physical file member. Just as a physical file member provides access to data by pointing to the data component of the physical file object, so also does the logical file member provide access by pointing to the physical file member. This is the way data access is achieved for the logical file.

It would be of little value to have a record format with fields and attributes defined in a file object, along with an access path, if there were no data. Yet, it is perfectly legitimate to do so with your AS/400 or IBM i.

Adding & Removing Members

From your experience in designing systems, you may have maintained batch job streams. These exist on all systems. During such job streams files are often created and deleted. Because the AS/400 is a database machine, and running the CRTPF command is the equivalent of a program compilation, there are two other ways to remove the data from a file without destroying the file itself.

The first is the Clear Physical File (CLRPFM) command. This command clears the referenced physical file member of all its data. If the file has but one member, then all data that was in the file, is gone. If you clear the data from a one member file, the data in the file is all cleared.

The other way of removing data from a member of a file is with the Remove Member (RMVM) command. This command removes the data component from the file. For a physical file, this means that the pointer to the data object is removed and the data space is reclaimed by the system. For a logical file, the pointer to the member in the physical file is removed and thus, the logical file cannot be used any longer to access the data in the physical file.

In batch streams where the RMVM technique is deployed, instead of the Delete File and Create File commands or the CLRPFM command, in order to fill the file with data again through the file object, you must add a member to the file. As you may expect, there are two Add Member commands available for your use. One is the Add Physical File Member (ADDPFM) command and the other is the Add Logical File Member (ADDLFM) command.

DDS to Build File Object

The DDS specifications for this physical database file are shown in Figure F-9. Before we study the DDS for this file, let's go over the format of the DDS specification form itself and also discuss the levels of keywords which are used to define various entities with the specifications.

Figure F-9 EARNMAST File With Headers (repeated)

```
type of DDS. All DDS statements have an A in column 6
|
|"*" means comment.  anything after * is treated as comment
| |
| |  "R" means that this is a Record Format; "K" means key field
| |   |
| |   | Names of Fields or Record Formats
| |   | |
| |   | |      Reference
| |   | |         |
| |   | |         | Data type and length
| |   | |         |  ||
| |   | |         |  || Number of decimal positions
| |   | |         |  || |
| |   | |         |  || |   Keywords
| |   | |         |  || |     |
VV    V V      V  VV V    V
A* Payroll Master
A*                            REF(HELLO/FIELDREF)
A     R  EARNMSTR             TEXT('Earnings Master')
         EMPNAM    25         COLHDG('Emp Name')
         EMPINL    2          COLHDG('Emp Initial')
         ACCT#     6  0       COLHDG('Account #')
         PAYCOD    1          COLHDG('Pay Code')
         RATE      6S 2
         STATUS    1          COLHDG('Pay Status')
         EMPNO     6  0
         MGRNO     6  0       COLHDG('Manager #')

A*       SAMPLE    R          REFFLD(FMT/SAMP HELLO/FIELDREF)

      K  EMPNO
```

...

Formal Diversion - Limited Database Theory

There is a notion in formal relational database design theory called Entity Relationship Diagraming E-R. Without getting into its detailed theory let me say that it has great value in helping design databases without anomalies. We'll get back to E-R shortly. Most all of us have heard of the notion of data base normalization. E-R and Data Normalization are complimentary theories and methodologies.

Data Base Normalization

Data base normalization can be summarized by this one cute phrase:

"Every field in a record design must depend on the key, the whole key and nothing but the key."

If you have a design which mirrors this statement then your data is probably, at least, in third normal form. When a field in a record does not depend on the primary key, then normalization rules dictate that the field and other fields that depend on the same field should be moved to a new file. That is one way in which files come into being – in formal data base design

Removing Repeating Groups

Another way files come into being is by removing repeating groups. When all repeating groups are removed, you have achieved first normal form. How do you remove repeating groups? First, you have to recognize the fields as repeating fields and secondly, you take them and move them to a new file. You create a new file for the repeating group.

So, how then do you think the Address Master and the Earnings Master and the Deduction Master came to being? If formal database design were used, they would come to being because of Database Normalization and Entity Relationship Diagraming.

Entities

Now, let's get a little technical for a little while. I will try to make this as painless as possible. Though we have not defined too much yet regarding Entity-Relationship (E-R) diagraming, and we won't be doing a lot of definition, we have been discussing some ways in which E-R can help us design databases and determine what goes into which file. Let's define a few things now that we have a general notion.

An entity can be defined as an object (not necessarily an IBM i object) that exists and is distinguishable from other objects. For instance, John Smith with Social Security Number (SSN) 490-11-2368 is an entity, as he can be uniquely identified by his social security number as one particular person in the universe. The notion of an entity is bigger than this, however. For example, an entity has various properties. An entity may be concrete such as a person or a car, or a magazine, for example or it can be abstract, such as a holiday or a concept, or an event.

An entity is represented by a set of attributes. An attribute can be thought of as a defining property. Attributes of a person include a name, a social security number, an employee number, etc. Attributes of a customer include a customer number, a street, a city, a credit limit, an amount owed, etc. You may recall at the beginning of chapter 2 that we acknowledged another name for a field or a column in a data base table. That name was none other than attribute. So the word has relevance in our study. Thus, a database attribute is a field in a database file. If entities are represented by attributes, then, it follows that the entities in a database are files, which some call tables and others call relations.

Entity Relationships

In E-R diagraming, as you would expect, the relationships among entities are diagramed, in an attempt to make sense of their various relationships in a relational database. The E-R diagram then, can be used as both a design tool and a map that shows how to use the data. Many designers believe that the construction of an Entity Relationship Diagram is essential for the design of tables, of extracts and even metadata (data about data). This book is intended to be a practical example-oriented tool for you to be able to learn and to work well with relational databases using DDS. E-R diagraming is beyond the scope of this book but it helps to know that in formal IT shops, such diagrams are the rule, not the exception.

Cardinality Relationships

E-R diagrams represent database files and the relationships among files. By having to diagram your database relationships before your design is complete, especially their cardinality relationships (one to one, one to many, etc.) you quickly get a perspective as to the shape your files should take.

Parent & Child Example

Whenever you have a one to one relationship of an attribute with an entity, you can expect that the attribute belongs with that particular entity. We can use a person entity (say a child) again as an example. A person has one first name. Therefore there is a one to one relationship of a person to a name. In database terms now, if we substitute the primary key (unique identifier) for a personnel record such as social security number, then we can say that the name has a one to one relationship with the primary key of social security number. For each SSN, you will have just one name.

Which Parent?

OK, now let's take a look at another attribute. How about parent's first name. Uh oh? Which parent? See the problem? There is a one to many relationship between the primary key (SSN) and the parent's first name. You may not like this example. You may say that at worse there is a one to two relationship - one child SSN to two parent sets of information. That's still one too many!

Am I Wrong?

You may challenge me by saying that there would be a one to one relationship if we had used mother's first name and father's first name instead of parent's first name. If we have a one to one relationship in database design, then the attribute belongs in the same record format as the primary key. If, on the other hand, we have a one to many relationship, then our data relationship modeling tells us we need to create a new file for the new entity which we have discovered — which is Parents. In database design, we devise a primary key for the parents (perhaps SSN again) and we move all of the associated information about the parents such as address information to the parent's file.

But, you may say, for a maximum of a one to two relationship, maybe we are better off keeping the parent's information in the child file. So maybe there are ten new fields we need to describe each parent which adds twenty fields to our database record. Maybe this is OK? But it is not relationally correct.

Parents Must Go!

Using the cardinality relationships of a one to many variety should be split into their own files. Now we see how files are called relations in relational database theory. Based on cardinality, the parents must go.

First Normal Form

How about the idea of first normal form, which says that there should be no repeating groups? Isn't two sets of ten fields a repeating group? According to first normal form, the Parent's gotta go!

Second and Third Normal Form

Second and third normal form (data normalization) start looking at each field, one by one, to be assured that each depends on the primary key. If we were walking through the parent's attributes in the child record (doesn't even sound right - does it?) , we might find a parent social security number and a parent street address.

Is the street address for the parent an attribute of the child?. No, it is not! It depends on the social security number (primary key - unique identifier) of the parent, not the social security number of the child. It does not depend on the primary key of the child entity, the whole key, and nothing but the key. Therefore, the second and/or third normal form test says that each of the parent's fields should be moved to a separate file so they can depend on the proper primary key for the proper entity.

Three For Three – Gotta Go!

So far, we are three for three against stuffing parent information in the child's file. Let's say you don't want a lot of files cluttering up your application and you go ahead and implement with the design as is. You do not create a Parent's file. Will it work? Well . . . maybe! But, it won't work well for parent things since parents remain a nonentity.

What About Divorce?

Now. Let us move the file into the twentieth century - the century where divorce became almost as common as marriage. Now what? You have designed two parent slots into your child record. What about mommy's new husband? Do you add ten more fields? What about daddy's new wife? Do you add another ten more fields? How many divorces are you going to permit each parent in your child database design? Can database design be the next big inhibitor to divorce? If it can, you may soon be on the Oprah Winfrey show!

Give Parents Own File

Of course, maybe it wasn't supposed to be there in the first place. Maybe you had a one to many relationship all along and maybe you should have designed for it – from the start! Give the parents their own file. Make sure that the primary key of the child is in each parent record. That way the data can be accessed from child or from parent. It's relational, right?

Many to Many Relationship

Is this really a many to many relationship? Whoah Nelly! That's one step up from a one to one relationship. Might a particular parent have more than one child? (That's any of the fifteen parents, to which you might have limited the child record in the prior design.) If this were a doctor's office or a hospital or a school or a church database application, would you expect that a parent might have more than one child involved. That's a many to many relationship. A parent may have many children and a child may have many parents. If we split the parents into their own file, this works both ways. Doesn't it? The many to many relationship is satisfied! Right?

Nope! It is not and it does not. The design works from child to parent since the common chord is child SSN. We are sticking it in each parent's record - regardless of how many parents. Unfortunately, it does not work the other way around — from parent to child. If there is a second child, it messes it up. The second child number cannot be rammed into the one child SSN slot in the parent record. Oh! Just add another child number to the parent record! That's a convenient solution. Whoops – the repeating group rule applies - No can do! Then what?

Just Make Some Rules?

Well! You could make rules such that the parents and the children have to use different doctors or go to different schools or hospitals but you know this would not work. If you could this, it might make a bad design last longer. You could use dummy social security numbers for a seconds set of records for the same parents - as many parents as there may be. You could relate the second child to the second set of parents through the new number. But, then you have data redundancy and you don't know that the second child and the first child are related. Wow! This gets complicated!

What Is the Solution?

How would you solve it? You could create a link file between the parents and the children. Its key would be a composite of the parents and the children's SSN. Each parent would have a field in the link record with his or her SSN and a child's SSN. The parent's number points to the parent information record. The child # points to the child information record. If a parent has four children that parent would have four records in the file. Each record in the link file would have the same parent SSN and the SSN of a different child. The beauty of this scenario is that you never run out of room. Another kid brings in another record in the link file. Another parent brings in another link.

What About the Kids?

What about the kids? If all the parent link records are completed, then all the kids' records are automatically completed! Right? "Yes, Indeedy!". If you were to sort the link file on the kids' SSN, most of them would probably have two records in the link file provided, one each, from each parent. Some may have one, some three, etc. depending on how many parents. This solves the parent child link! But does it do it well?

How do we link child to child? This starts to hurt my head at this point. Can you use the parent/child link file for this? Theoretically you can! You could join sibling records with parent records. The view of the join could have a child's SSN, parents SSN, and a record in the file for each of the siblings of each parent. For each child in a join like this, there would be enough records to handle each parent and all of the siblings of each parent. Since, by definition, there would be duplicates in the view in that a brother would show up under both parents, as would his sister, there would be some additional tuning necessary. But, the deed is theoretically accomplishable. Don't ask me to code the DDS for this now. But, it would be fun! By the way, there is an example coming up which shows how to join a file with itself, which, in essence we would be doing in this situation.

Since it hurts all of our heads to go there, we will stop here and say that — if you read all this, you have an appreciation for database design and how important it is – even if you don't know it all . . . yet!

Different Methods Can Be Used

Just a few more comments now before the pain is over completely. There are many ways to skin a briefcase. Being bits and bytes efficient is not always the right approach. For example, a child - child file might be the best bet in addition to the parent-child file. All the machinations to join a file to itself and then to other records may not be worth the pain and the performance. In this file, you could have the SSN of each child on the left and right side of a table. SS#1 may have four records with SS#1 and SS#2, SS#1 and SS#3,

One final note regarding the parent information file and the child information file. Theoretically, they can be one file. If SSN is the key, remember that a file can be joined to itself and the link file could be joined twice to the same parent/child file. As long as all the records are the same. If we did this, of course, we would no longer have a parent entity, we would have a person entity instead and we would have to classify people as child or parent or both. It would become so much fun that you might even say, "two files are better. That idea doesn't hurt my head."

Many of the design situations you get into can hurt your head. It is always best to keep the design simple and understandable. The next time you look at your own DB work, if it is complex, it may take you a long time to come up to speed to understand your own design. The other possibility, of course is that you won't necessarily see anomalies right away and if you implement with unseen data anomalies, you will get big time headaches.

Chapter 7   DDS Levels a.k.a. the DDS Hierarchy

Using DDS for Describing Databases

DDS is a method of describing data base files, communications files, display formats, and printer files to the system. The user enters DDS in source code format (typically with SEU into QDDSSRC) to describe the file, then compiles the source code to produce a database file that can be used by the system.

The database DDS source statements describe the length of each field, field attributes (character or numeric), the name of the field, etc. Once the DDS source is entered, the user invokes the file creation process (CRTPF or CRTLF), which uses the DDS to build the database file object.

In this sense, you can think of files as being "compiled" on the AS/400, just the way programs are compiled. Source statements are entered into the system, transformed into a file object that can be used in a program. Unlike normal compiler operations, the compiler derives the description of the file from DDS, not from COBOL or RPG specifications. When the file descriptions are used in programs, they are referred to as "externally described" files.

The DDS Hierarchy

We will review the DDS specification form layout in detail below, but first, let us again examine the structure of how DDS is built within the context of the DDS form. As we previously discussed in general terms in Chapter 4, under the heading The Six Levels of DDS, it helps to remember that DDS organization is by field, by record format, and by file. What does this mean? It means simply that there are certain things that you can prescribe for the file itself. You can prescribe other rules for the record formats, and you can select still other rules for the fields. When used in this context, these rules are called file level, record level, and field level attributes. There are also three other levels used when defining keys or selection criteria. These are aptly called: Key-Field Level, Select/Omit level, and Join Record Level.

At the file level, sometimes the attributes pertain just for the file. However, sometimes their placement at the file level in DDS means that they apply to all of the formats and fields within the file. Thus lower levels inherit from higher levels. The same applies to formats. Some attributes may pertain just to the format itself, while other attributes, though prescribed at the record format level, may pertain also to the data fields. Though the cascading notion of levels does apply to physical and logical files, it is most visible in display files.

Let's define our terms before proceeding any further:

Level Description

Field:

> A Field is a column in a table such as NAME, ADDRESS, PHONE, etc. Use DDS to specify the type and length. Examples of keywords specified at the field level:

> RANGE-- Data entered must be within ranges
> VALUES--Data entered must be in list

Record
Format:

A record format is a logical grouping of fields which can
be referenced by the name of the record format.
Examples of keywords specified at the record format
level:

FORMAT --Record format is to share the field specs
(record layout / names etc.) of a previously defined
record format.

PFILE – For logical files, the "underlying" physical file.

Join Record
Format:

A Join Record Format gives the system information
about the shape of the record. The record comprises
fields from multiple physical files when used in a join
logical file. his is the DDS level in which you would
join a number of physical files.

File:

Files are composed of one or more record formats.
Keywords at the file level are optional. Examples of the
keywords specified at the file level:

PRINT – "Print" key allowed on this display
UNIQUE – Data base keys must be unique
INDARA – Print File Indicator Area used

Key
Field:

Key field entries are specified at the key-field level.
These entries reference fields previously defined in the
DDS member and designate those fields as key fields by
having a "K" in column 17. Examples of the keywords
specified at the Key-field level:

DESCEND--Records are arranged in descending
sequence
LIFO -- Records are presented in LIFO sequence

Select/
Omit:

Select/Omit level entries are specified at the select/omit
level. These entries reference fields previously defined
in the DDS member and designate those fields by having
an "S" for   select, or an "O" for omit. Through these
entries logical files are given their ability to select records
(or omit). Examples of the keywords specified at the
select/omit level are:

COMP--Records which compare to the value
specified in this keyword are selected or omitted.
RANGE-- Records which are within the range
specified are selected or omitted.

Additional DDS Insights

Looking at this in hierarchical form, there are three distinct
major levels. Two of the levels even have sub-levels. Thee three
different levels of information in the hierarchy and the
associated sub-levels are as follows

1. Field --Field, key field, S/O field
2. Record--Record format, Join record format
3. File--File

For special functions, there are two additional field sublevels levels known as the key-field level, and the select/omit level. These both use fields to change the selection and order of records.

Fields are grouped together to form record formats. Fields in a join view are grouped together to form a join record format. One or more record formats can be grouped to form a file. This is an important concept. Once you've got that down, it is much easier to understand that different DDS keywords apply at the different levels in the hierarchy. In fact, some keywords can actually be used at more than one level. A simple example of this is the TEXT keyword.

How Do You Specify the Level of a Keyword?

It's actually easier than trying to explain it. Keywords that are specified before the first record format name ("R" in 17) in DDS are file level keywords. Keywords specified from the record format to the first field of the format are record-level keywords. Keywords specified from one field, to before the next field, a.k.a. between fields are field level keywords for that field. Keywords between the last field and the end of DDS or until the first key field or select/omit field are also field level keywords. Keywords that have a "K" in column 17 and are specified after all fields in a record format are known as key-field level keywords. If, instead of a "K," they happen to have an "S" or an "O" or a blank, they are known as select/omit keywords.

The following is a brief list of some popular keywords along with a short description of the keyword and an indication of the level(s) at which it can be specified. These keywords are frequently used in DDS to describe both database files and display files.

TEXT:

Enter text of your choice to describe your file, record format, or field (all levels, all file types)

COLHDG:

Column heading. The words you enter here will be shown as the default column headings when you use Query or other AS/400 utilities (field-level keyword in physical files)

ALIAS:

For COBOL programmers, DDS allows you to enter 10 byte names. If you would like to use longer names, ALIAS provides a means. (field-level, physical file)

REF:

Reference. Specify the name of another file containing the type and length for this field. This allows you to standardize your field definitions. (file-level, all types)

COMP:

Compare. For data base files, this keyword allows you to select or omit certain records. For example, COMP(EQ 'MI') might be used to select those records where the state is Michigan. (field level for display file, select/omit-level for a logical file)

EDTCDE:

Edit Code. Use this keyword to edit your numeric output by including dollar signs, decimal points, commas, etc. (field level)

PFILE:

The "based-on" physical file. Use this keyword at the record level of a logical file to designate the based on physical file (record level)

There are literally tons of database DDS keywords available to provide you with a wide variety of functions for your database files. In just a few pages, as you are being introduced to columnar nature of the DDS form, you will see that the DDS keywords are specified beginning in column 45 of the form as shown in Figure F-9. In this section all of the DDS keywords are listed.

☐ Hint: Figure F-9 is first shown in Chapter 6 and is repeated in Chapter 8 for your convenience.

☐ Hint: IBM's DDS manual DDS Reference: Physical and Logical Files has excellent explanations and examples for all of the keywords shown. You can use the appendix in this book to help you locate and download this and other valuable IBM i manuals from the IBM Web site.

You need not master them all at once to be effective in using the system's data base and device capabilities. A keyword a day . . . will help. The above list represents just a few keywords that you will master early in your AS/400 experience . . . perhaps even later on today . . . but surely soon . . .

Chapter 8   The DDS Specification for Database Files

The Data Description Specification (DDS) Form

Now, let us explore the DDS form from top to bottom and from column to column – without skipping any columns.

DDS Column 6 - Form Designator

As you can see in Figure F-9, repeated below for your convenience, the DDS specification is designed with an "A" in column six for the form type. This fits into the same general model as used in the RPG language specification forms. They too use column six as the defining form ID.

From all I have studied about DDS, I have found no apparent rhyme or reason for IBM's selection of an "A." for the DDS form type. RPG/400 for example, uses "F" for file description, "I" for input, "C" for calculations, etc. These make sense. An "A" for DDS does not make sense. It would be more logical for the DDS form type designator to be a "D." Unfortunately, this will never happen since, some fifteen years after designing the DDS form, IBM used the "D" designation in its definition of ILE RPG (a.k.a. RPGIV). It is the RPG IV data definition specification. Regardless of its origin, all DDS specifications can be differentiated from other IBM specifications by the presence of an "A" in column six.

Figure F-9 EARNMAST File With Headers (repeated)

```
type of DDS. All DDS statements have an A in columne 6
|
|"*" means comment. anything after * is treated as comment
||
||   "R" means that this is a Record Format; "K" means key field
||   |
||   |   Names of Fields or Record Formats
||   |   |
||   |   |       Reference
||   |   |           |
||   |   |           | Data type and length
||   |   |           | ||
||   |   |           | || Number of decimal positions
||   |   |           | || |
||   |   |           | || |   Keywords
||   |   |           | || |   |
VV   V V         V  VV V    V
A* Payroll Master
A*                          REF(HELLO/FIELDREF)
A    R  EARNMSTR            TEXT('Earnings Master')
        EMPNAM    25        COLHDG('Emp Name')
        EMPINL    2         COLHDG('Emp Initial')
        ACCT#     6  0      COLHDG('Account #')
        PAYCOD    1         COLHDG('Pay Code')
        RATE      6S 2
        STATUS    1         COLHDG('Pay Status')
        EMPNO     6  0
        MGRNO     6  0      COLHDG('Manager #')

A*      SAMPLE    R         REFFLD(FMT/SAMP HELLO/FIELDREF)

     K  EMPNO
        ...
```

As a point of note, you may have already noticed that a number of the DDS statements in Figure F-9 do not have an "A" in column six. When the DDS database compilers (CRTPF or CRTLF) are used, they assume that all statements have an A in column six. If you do not put an "A" in column six, the compiler forgives you.

DDS Column 7 - Comments

Column seven is used for denoting a particular statement as a comment. Comments are used in DDS for readability and for documentation. If there is an "*" in column seven, instead of a DDS specification, the statement is considered a comment line and thus, it does not provide any input to the file creation process.

DDS Columns 8 to 16 - Unused

Columns 8 through 16 are very easy to explain. You can put your brain to sleep since these columns are not used for describing database files.

DDS Column 17 –

Type of Name or Specification for Physical and Logical Files

If you took my advice, it's already time to wake up. You must be careful as to what you place in column 17. It will take some study to understand what all the options actually do. In this column, you place the type of name or specification for physical and logical files. Keep in mind that different types of statements mean different kinds of things. Since all DDS uses an A in column six as the DDS designator, IBM chose column 17 to serve as a means of differentiating various types of DDS specifications.

The best way to describe what this all means is to list the various codes which can be placed in column 17 and their meanings. If the specification refers to a name, such as a format name or a field name, the name is entered in positions 19 through 28.

The valid entries in column 17 for physical files are as follows:

Entry	Meaning
R	Record format name
Blank	Field name
K	Key field name

You can specify just one "R" for a physical file since a physical file has but one format.

The valid column 17 entries for logical files are:

Entry	Meaning
R	Record format name
J	Join specification
Blank	Field name or select/omit AND condition
K	Key field name
S	Select field name
O	Omit field name

Logical files can have more than one "R" designation since a logical file can be built over multiple physical files. Each of the "R" record formats from the underlying physical files can exist in the logical file. We will discuss this topic in greater detail in the Join DDS examples beginning in Chapter 16.

The DDS examples also demonstrate how and when to use the "J" for joining physical files, K for sequencing (ORDERING) files, as well as the "S" for selecting records and the "O" for omitting records in a logical view.

DDS Column 18 - Unused

IBM did not forget position 18 in the form. However, it remains unused for all file types created with DDS.

DDS Columns 19 to 28 –

Name for Physical and Logical Files

Positions 19 through 28, as noted above, are used to name the item you have designated in column 17. For example, if you specify an "R" in 17, you will specify the name of the record format in columns 19 through 28. If you specify a blank, the name represents a field name within the record. If you specify a

"J," it is the name you are giving to a join record format. If you specify a "K," you put the name of the key field in these positions. If you specify an "S" or an "O," the name represents the field you are testing for record selection or omission.

Column 17 and columns 19 through 28 are closely related. In columns 19 through 28, you enter the name for elements in physical and logical files such as fields and record formats. Column 17 says what type of name you are specifying. In summary, you will use these positions to specify names for the following:

1. Record Format   The record format ('R' in 17) for this physical file or formats for this logical file

2. Join Record Format: The record format name in a logical file which joins records from one or more physical files.

3. Field: The field name or field names that make up the record format (unless you specify the FORMAT or PFILE keyword at the record level – Format and PFILE are described later in this book)

4. Key Field: The field or fields used as key fields

5. Select / Omit: For logical files, the field or fields to be used for select/omit specifications

DDS Column 29 –

Reference for Physical and Logical Files

Position 29 is the spot in the form where you specify the reference file information for physical files. For a logical file, you would leave this position blank. All logical files automatically provide the reference capability for all specified fields. In other words, any attributes that are not specified explicitly in the logical file are furnished from the corresponding field in the physical file record format with no additional work.

☐ Hint: Field Reference Files are described in Chapter 4 under the heading: Field Reference File – Data Dictionary.

For a physical file, as you will see in the coding examples, you must specify an "R" for "reference" in position 29 if you want the DDS compiler to use the attributes of a previously defined field (called the referenced field). You must also specify the REF keyword at the file level or the REFFLD keyword at the field level to tell the compiler the file and/or field which you are using as a reference. The field can come from a reference file (REF keyword) or from a field within the set of DDS being entered (REFFLD) or from a field in a file as specified on the REFFLD keyword.

DDS Columns 39 to 34 –

Field Length for Physical and Logical Files

Positions 30 through 34 are used to specify the field length for physical and logical files. For a physical file, you use these positions to specify the field length for each named field which does not get its length and attributes from a reference file. In this column space, you specify the number of digits for a numeric type field or the number of characters for a character type field.

For a logical file, you could use these positions to specify the length of a logical field as seen through the view. You would specify the length in logical file DDS only if you wished to override or change the length of the corresponding field in the physical file on which this logical file is based.

DDS Column 35 –

Data type for Physical and Logical Files

For a physical file, you use this position to specify the data type of the field within the database. For a logical file, specify the data type only to override or change the data type of the corresponding field in the physical file on which the logical file is based.

If you leave this position blank, the field you are defining has the same data type as the corresponding field in the physical file(s) upon which the logical file is based.
Valid data type entries are as follows:

Entry	Meaning
P	Packed decimal
S	Zoned decimal
B	Binary
F	Floating-point
A	Character
H	Hexadecimal
L	Date
T	Time
Z	Timestamp

The default data type (blank) is alphabetic (character). For numeric data types, if the S or P designation is not selected, a length and decimal positions entry for the field will default to packed decimal.

☐ Hint: Packed decimal is an internal data representation for numeric data. The AS/400 and IBM i are optimized for performing internal operations with packed decimal fields. Thus, data stored in the data base is converted to packed decimal before numeric operations are applied. Packed decimal also saves space on disk.

The formula for disk space savings is as follows: Divide the number of digits required to store a value by two, then add one and round up. For example, if 10 digits were required to store a value, if we were to divide the number 10 by 2 we would get five. If we add one to five, we get six. Thus, using packed decimal format, we could store a ten-digit number in only six memory positions.

Even though there is a definite savings in disk storage, and there is less processor overhead with packed decimal, today most database designers choose not to use it. Why? Computers are faster than ever. Disk space is less expensive than ever. More importantly, packed values are not as easy to deal within debugging data errors as full signed numeric. Additionally, Query users do not relate well to packed decimal data in database files. Since the human time spent in any phase of a project is far more costly than machine time, packed decimal has fallen out of favor. But, that does not mean you will not find it in home grown code and/or packages in your shops.

DDS Columns 36 to 37 –

of Decimal Places for Physical and Logical Files

Positions 36 and 37. Specify the number of decimal positions for physical and logical files in columns 36 and 37. For a physical file, use these positions to specify the decimal placement within a packed decimal, zoned decimal, binary, or floating-point field. Specify a decimal number from 0 through 31 for the number of decimal positions to the right of the decimal point. For logical files, specify decimal positions only to override or change the decimal positions of the corresponding field in the physical file upon which the logical file is based.

DDS Column 38 - Unused

Position 38 does not have to be filled in.

DDS Columns 39 to 44 - Unused

Positions 39 through 44 do not apply to Physical or logical files. Leave them blank.

DDS Columns 45 to 80 - Keywords

Positions 45 through 80. This is the area of the DDS form in which keyword entries for physical and logical files are specified. This section is the area in which you put the keyword entries which are valid for describing physical and logical files.

Keywords

DDS is keyword driven. Though the specification for which we just described does accommodate certain attributes of fields and records such as length and decimal positions, the real action comes about through the use of the keywords which are specified from column 45 to 80 in the DDS form.

Since certain keywords are valid for just physical files and certain keywords are valid for just logical files, and other keywords are valid for both physical and logical files, for better understanding, have split out the keywords along these groupings.

Keywords for Both Physical and Logical Files

The following keywords are valid for both physical and logical files (except where noted):

ABSVAL	ALIAS
ALL (logical files only)	ALTSEQ
ALWNULL (physical only	CCSID (physical only)
CHECK	CHKMSGID
CMP	COLHDG
COMP	CONCAT (logical only)
DATFMT	DATSEP
DESCEND	DFT (physical only)
DIGIT	DYNSLT (logical only)
EDTCDE	EDTWRD
FCFO	FIFO
FLTPCN	FORMAT
LIFO	NOALTSEQ
RANGE	REF (physical only)
REFFLD (physical only)	REFSHIFT
RENAME (logical only)	SIGNED
SST (logical only)	TEXT
TIMFMT	TIMSEP
TRNTBL (logical only)	UNIQUE
UNSIGNED	VALUES
VARLEN	ZONE

Keywords for Logical Files

Beginning in Chapter 12, we discuss the notion of simple, multiple format, and join logical files. We have separated the logical file keywords into two groupings since that is how the keywords line up

Keywords for Simple and Multiple Format Logical Files

The following keywords are valid only for simple and multiple format logical files:

PFILE   REFACCPTH

Keywords for Join Logical Files

The following keywords are valid only for join logical files:

JDFTVAL   JDUPSEQ
JFILE   JFLD
JOIN   JREF

Exceptions for Source Files

Because of the inherent nature of source programs and the tricks built into the Source Entry Utility (SEU) editor to assure that source is handled in the fashion intended by the programmer, there are restrictions in the use of various keywords when used to create source files. Though the Create Source Physical File (CRTSRCPF) command is typically used to create source files, you can build your own source files without using this IBM convention.

Building Source Files with DDS

When you create a source file with no DDS using the above command, you specify the record length for the source file. The value must include 6 bytes for the source sequence number and 6 bytes for the date. If no value is specified, 92 (6 + 6 + 80) is used as the default. The system builds you a three field externally described physical file with a *NOMAX number of members and other source-file-appropriate database values.

Though the file is intended for source programs, you can store data in the file if you wish, since all source files are database files. Valid record length values range from 13 through 32766 bytes.

If you were to use the command Display File Field Description (DSPFFD) against a default source file, you would find the following three field definitions:

Field	Data Type	Field Length		Buffer Length	Buffer Position
SRCSEQ	ZONED	6	2	6	1
SRCDAT	ZONED	6	0	6	7
SRCDTA	CHAR	80		80	13

You can create your own source file using the Create Physical File command if you specify three fields in DDS. As long as they are named exactly as above, and as they all have the same attributes, and as long as the first two fields (SRCSEQ and SRCDAT) are defined with exactly the same length and decimal positions as shown above. The SRCDTA field can be as big as 32, 766   minus 12.

You can create a source file with DDS since that is basically what IBM does under the covers anyway. However, there are keyword restrictions for source files since SEU cannot guarantee that the file will behave as a source file if you specify DDS keywords which would cause the source programs to lose track of the proper order of the statements. If keywords caused the beginning to be the end and there was no integrity to the sequencing of the source statements, this would not prove to be productive for your shop.

When you use DDS to describe a source file (usually created without DDS, using the CRTSRCPF command) or even when a logical file is based on a physical file which is to be used as a source file, you cannot use the following keywords because the integrity of the source cannot be guaranteed, and in some cases is assured of being incorrect.

ABSVAL	ALTSEQ
DESCEND	FCFO
FIFO	LIFO
NOALTSEQ	SIGNED
UNIQUE	VARLEN
ZONE	

Why are Certain Keywords Excluded?

Consider, if an alternate collating sequence were used and statement four became statement seven. How about if you used FIFO (first -in, first out). Suppose you changed a statement in the middle of the program. The FIFO rule would permit duplicate source statement numbers and it would arrange the duplicates in arrival sequence regardless of intention. Think about what DESCEND (descending order) would do to the integrity of your program. Therefore, since SEU cannot guarantee integrity if you use these keywords, you should not use them. If you can, it is better to use the IBM-supplied CRTSRCPF command since it takes all of these things into consideration and is much easier to use than DDS.

DDS Examples

Many of the DDS examples which we are about to present - and there are lots of them use a simple file definition which we have labeled EARNMAST, It has a Payroll application basis but is substantially smaller than a typical payroll master record. This is the same file object we examined in Chapter 6.

In addition to the EARNMAST file, later on, in a different chapter of this QuikCourse, we will be needing several other file definitions. The record layout for the EARNMAST file, the ADDRMAST File, the DEDMAST File and the TIMECD file are all given as follows: follows:

EARNMAST Payroll Earnings File

Field Name	Description	From/To	Type	L/Dec	
EARNMSTR	Record format name	NA			
EMPNAM	Employee Name	1 to 25	Alpha	25	
EMPINL	Employee Initial	26 to 27	Alpha	2	
ACCT#	Payroll ACCT #	28 to 31	NumP	6 / 0	*
PAYCOD	Payl code (S- sal.H-hrly)	32 to 32	Alph	1	
RATE	Pay rate	33 to 38	NumS	6 / 2	**
STATUS	Payroll Status (A-Act, I -IN)	39 to 39	Alpha	1	
EMPNO	Employee Number (key)	40 to 43	NumP	6 / 0	*
MGRNO	Manager Number (in EARN)	44 to 47	NumP	6 / 0	*
SALARY	Employee Salary if salaried	48 to 55	NumS	8 / 2	**

ADDRMAST Payroll Name / Address Master File

Field Name	Description	From/To	Type	L/Dec	
ADDRMSTR	Record format name	NA			
EMPNO	Employee Number (key)	1 to 4	NumP	6 / 0	*
LINE#	Address Line Number	5 to 6	NumS	2 / 0	**
ADLINE	Address Line Data	7 to 46	Alph	40	
	*				

DEDMAST Payroll Deduction Master File

Field Name	Description	From/To	Type	L/Dec	
DEDMSTR	Record format name	NA			
EMPNO	Employee Number (key)	1 to 4	NumP	6 / 0	*
DEDTYP	Deduction Type	5 to 9	Alph	5	
DEDDSC	Deduction Description	10 to 39	Alph	40	
DEDAMT	Deduction Amount	50 to 43	NumP	6 / 2	*
DEDFRQ	Deduction Frequency	54 to 45	NumS	2 / 0	**

TIMECD Payroll Time Card Transaction File

Field Name	Description	From/To	Type	L/Dec	
TIMECDR	Record format name	NA			
EMPNO	Employee Number (key)	1 to 6	numP	6 / 0	*
PAYPRD	Yearly Pay Period	7 to 8	Alph	2	
HOURS	Hourse Worked	9 to 14	NumP	6 / 2	*

* P = packed decimal numeric
* S = Signed decimal numeric

You may have noticed that the four numeric fields in EARNMAST – ACCT#, RATE, and EMPNO have two different letter designations after the num. In this example NumP means that this field is compressed using IBM's packed decimal format. Quite simply IBM can fit two numeric digits in one storage position using this format. Since ½ position is required for the sign of the field, you can calculate the number of storage positions required to store a packed number by dividing the length of the field by two and adding one.

EMPNO, for example is six positions long with no decimals. Six divided by two is three – plus one is four. Thus the six digits in EMPNO fit nicely into the four positions (39-42) of the record layout.

The RATE field is coded as NumS. In this example, this means that the six positions of the RATE will take six positions of storage. Since half of each position is not being used in this case, here is plenty of room for IBM to put the sign of the field. When we explain the DDS below, we will go over this again in the context of the DDS.

Creating the EARNMAST File

The DDS or this file is shown in Figure F-9. The DDS in Figure F-9 has a ton of columnar descriptive information prior to the actual coding. In this way, you can visualize what the DDS looks like – all nicely typed up. For all of the other examples in this chapter, we will abbreviate this description for space purposes. Thank you for your understanding.

The DDS for the EARNMAST file is shown in Figure F-9.

Figure F-9 EARNMAST File With Headers

```
type of DDS. All DDS statements have an A in columne 6
|
|"*" means comment. anything after * is treated as comment
||
||  "R" means that this is a Record Format; "K" means key field
||    |
||    |  Names of Fields or Record Formats
||    |  |
||    |  |            Reference
||    |  |              |
||    |  |              |  Data type and length
||    |  |              |  ||
||    |  |              |  || Number of decimal positions
||    |  |              |  || |
||    |  |              |  || |    Keywords
||    |  |              |  || |      |
VV    V  V         V   VV V    V
A* Payroll Master
A*                                REF(HELLO/FIELDREF)
A     R  EARNMSTR                 TEXT('Earnings Master')
         EMPNAM    25             COLHDG('Emp Name')
         EMPINL     2             COLHDG('Emp Initial')
         ACCT#      6  0          COLHDG('Account #')
         PAYCOD     1             COLHDG('Pay Code')
         RATE      6S 2
         STATUS     1             COLHDG('Pay Status')
         EMPNO      6  0
         MGRNO      6  0          COLHDG('Manager #')
         SALARY    8S 2           COLHDG('Employee Salary')

A*       SAMPLE    R              REFFLD(FMT/SAMP HELLO/FIELDREF)

      K  EMPNO
         ...
```

You may already have noticed that we used very small field
names for DDS – 6 characters in fact. These were kept small to
fit RPG/400 coding conventions. The newer RPGIV, which is
becoming more and more accepted permits larger definitions.

There are not that many unique attributes to get all fussed up
about when creating a simple physical database file. You can
see the record format named EARNMSTR in Figure F-9.
Notice that there is a TEXT record level keyword associated
with it to help document the record.

Following the record format is the first field definition for
employee name EMPNAM which has an unspecified data type
(blank). This means that the default "character" applies so this
is a character field of length 25. Moving down the list of fields,

you can see the filed named: RATE. This is defined as "6S 2". The data type is listed as "S" meaning signed numeric, and the number of decimal places is listed as two. This field will take up six spaces in the record and the last two spaces will be for the decimal positions.

If you contrast this definition with that of the field EMPNO below it, you can see that EMPNO has no data type specified. The default for a field with decimals specified (0 in this case) and no data type specified is numeric. However, in the database, default fields are stored in packed decimal format so that a six-position field takes up only four spaces in the database. The space formula is ((field length / 2) + 1). This is an IBM space saving mechanism for using both halves of a byte for numeric data. Most IBM processors actually perform arithmetic on data in this form, so it is a very common data form. Though RATE and EMPNUM are both six positions, the data is shaped differently when the "S" is used as opposed to taking the numeric default of packed decimal.

The last field in the file is called MGRNO. This is the employee number of the employee's manager. To find the name of the manager, if you were writing a program, you would read the employee record in EARNMAST, get the MGRNO, and re-access the file with MGRNO as the search argument. The second time you got a record from the file, the EMPNAM field would be filled with the manager's name. It would be the manager's name. We have a special join near the end of the book which does this with a logical view. You'll like it.

Chapter 9   Example DDS - Physical File Coding

DDS Solutions

In this next set of chapters, we present specific database solutions built with DDS. Some will be very simple. Some will be somewhat complicated. Others may at first seem simple, but will stretch your knowledge to understand the new notions inherent in the examples. The examples in the next few chapters may help you find that this little DDS guide can be a valuable tool to keep with you as your handy pocket database reference to developing many different database solutions.

Keyword Levels

In Chapter 7, we covered the idea of the various DDS levels and how they work, without doing any coding in DDS. Now, we will demonstrate the various levels while by coding various level Physical File DDS keywords.

Take a look at Figure F-10 for another look at the keyword levels in DDS. You will see that the DDS in Figure F-10 is a smaller version of Figure F-9, which introduced the EARNMAST physical file. To make it even more helpful, Figure F-10 has all the levels marked within the DDS form itself.

Figure F-10 Keyword Levels for EARNMAST

```
                                   File Level
A* Payroll Master
A     R  EARNMSTR                  Record Level
                                   Record Level

         EMPNAM      25  0         Field Level
                                   Field Level
         EMPINL       2
         ACCT#        6  0
         PAYCOD       1
         RATE        6S  2
         STATUS       1
         EMPNO        6  0

      K  EMPNO                         Key Level
      S  PAYCOD         ... COMP(.. Select/Omit Level

      ...
```

Specifying File Level PF Keywords

Now take a look at Figures F-11 and F-12. You can see there
are examples of File level keywords for physical files, in action.
In these two figures, you can see how keywords such as
ALTSEQ, FIFO, LIFO, REF, and UNIQUE are specified at
the file level.

Figure F-11, File Level Keywords in Action

```
A* DDS Physical File (W/ FIELD REFERENCE file)
A* PHYSICAL FILE (EARNMAST)
A*
A                                  REF(FIELDREF)
A                                  UNIQUE
A     R  EARNMSTR                  TEXT('Earnings Master')
         EMPNAM       R
         EMPINL       R
         ACCT#        R
         PAYCOD       R
         RATE         R
         STATUS       R

         EMPNO        6  0  <- not a particularly good
                                coding technique
         SALARY       R
      K  EMPNO
            . . .
```

Coding Technique

In Figure F-11, in addition to specifying the REF and UNIQUE file level keywords, we added a note (not a valid DDS comment) on the EMPNO field statement. The note suggests that this is not a particularly good coding technique. It is not! When you choose to have a field reference file serve as your application "dictionary" for field names, it does not make sense, in most cases, to explicitly define a field within your DDS.

☐ Hint: In Chapter 4, you can get a lot more information on AS/400 physical files as data dictionaries and field reference files. Look under the heading Field Reference File - Data Dictionary

Ironically, the only DDS statement that was in the form that we have been using is the EMPNO field. All of the other fields have an "R" code for reference in column 29 of the DDS form. There is no REFFLD keyword so the field name in the reference file is the same name as the field which is being referenced. If it is not, of course, there will be a big error. .

REF & UNIQUE

The first keyword – REF(FIELDREF)in the whole set of DDS is specified at the file level. Thus, it pertains to all formats in the physical file DDS as well as all fields in the DDS. The five fields, EMPNAM, EMPINL ACCT#, PAYCOD, and RATE all are coded with an "R" in 29 which tells the DDS compiler to go to the file specified with the REF keyword (FIELDREF) to get the actual definition for the particular field. As you can see this technique saves keying and, though it might not be as obvious, it also helps assure field size and attribute standardization.

The file level keywords used in the example are REF and UNIQUE. As already noted, REF specifies the name of the field reference file or other physical file from which field descriptions are to be retrieved. UNIQUE specifies that there are no duplicate employee # keys allowed for this physical database file.

Figure F-12A Additional File Level Keywords for Physical Files

```
A* PHYSICAL FILE (EARNMAST)
A*
A                                   ALTSEQ(TABLELIB/TABLE1)
A                                   FIFO or LIFO or FCFO
A      R  EARNMSTR                  TEXT('Earnings Master')
          EMPNAM    R
          EMPINL    R
          ACCT#     R
          PAYCOD    R
          RATE      R
          STATUS    R
          EMPNO     R
          SALARY    R

       K  EMPNO
          . . .
```

Catch the Error?

In Figure F-12A, you can see that we added a few extra keywords at the file level and we corrected the poor coding technique as outlined in Figure F-11. All fields use the "R" code so that their definitions will come from the REF file. Whoops! We did not specify the REF keyword. Thus, this set of DDS would not fly. It would be DOA at the DDS compiler stop. You would need to add the REF keyword as in Figure F-10 for this DDS to compile cleanly.

Alternate Collating Sequence

In Figure F-12A, we also demonstrate how to specify an alternate sequence table. To create the table, you would use the CRTTBL command. You would create an alternate sequence if you wanted certain characters to be "appear differently in the collating sequence. For example, if you wanted a B to appear before an A. You would change their positioning in the table.

The AS/400 command CRTTBL is shown below with the proper parameters to obtain a prompt panel (Figure 12-B) which enables the modification of the sequencing tables.

CRTTBL TBL(HELLO/TABLE1) SRCFILE(*PROMPT) TBLTYPE(*SRTSEQ)

When you type this command on your AS/400 command line, you will get a panel similar to that in Figure F-12B.

Figure F-12B Create an Alternate Sequence Table

```
                          Create Sort Sequence

Table:    TABLE1          Library:   HELLO
Stored in CCSID value:    37

Type sequence number (0-9999) for each character, press Enter.
(Use the same sequence number to have characters sort in
a group.)

Sequence  Char     Sequence  Char     Sequence  Char     Sequence  Char
  0010              0110    .            0210    í          0310    □
  0020    â         0120    <            0220    î          0320    ─
  0030    ä         0130    (            0230    ï          0330    /
  0040    à         0140    +            0240    ì          0340    Â
  0050    á         0150    |            0250    ß          0350    Ä
  0060    ã         0160    &            0260    !          0360    À
  0070    å         0170    é            0270    $          0370    Á
  0080    ç         0180    ê            0280    *          0380    Ã
  0090    ñ         0190    ë            0290    )          0390    Å
  0100    ¢         0200    è            0300    ;          0400    Ç

More...
F3=Exit              F5=Refresh    F6=Create    F11=Hex characters    F12=Cancel
F17=Position to      F20=Renumber
```

From the panel in Figure 12-B, you can alter the sequence of characters so that certain characters are collated after or before other specified characters. If you find a need for an alternate collating sequence for a database, this command is very helpful and there is an ample supply of help available for nuances you may need to add. Most folks will never find a need for this facility.

FIFO, LIFO, FCFO

In Figure F-12A, you can also see the keywords, FIFO (First in, first out), LIFO (Last in, first out) and FCFO (First changed, first out). These are handy ways to tell the system what you would like done if there are duplicate keys. You tell the system to arrange the records in the order in which they came in, the reverse order in which they arrived, or by when they were changed.

Since no other relational database, of which I am aware, supports the notion of duplicate keys (non-unique primary keys), this is either a major plus for those who like additional facility or it is a major minus for those who want all databases to behave exactly the same. As you may have already surmised, these access rules may come in very handy in an inventory costing application where a LIFO or FIFO method is appropriate.

Specifying Record Level PF Keywords

Figure F-13 shows examples of two different Physical File Record Level keywords, TEXT and FORMAT. This code will not work because of keyword conflicts. It is shown to demonstrate the placement of the keywords.

Figure F-13 Record Level PF Keywords

```
A      R   EARNMSTR                    FORMAT(PMASTER)
                                       TEXT('Earnings Master')
A*         EMPNAM    R   (Fields are not allowed with FORMAT)

A      R   COURSE                      TEXT('Course Format')
           COURS#    R

TEXT
```

The "TEXT" keyword is very easy to explain. For any record that you want to document, you can specify the TEXT keyword and type a short description. The description is captured within the object description when the database is compiled.

FORMAT

Format is a bit more difficult. You would use this record-level keyword in both physical and logical files to specify that this record format is to share the field specifications from a previously defined record format in an already compiled file object. When choosing to use this developer's timesaving mechanism, you must remember that the name you provide for your record format ("R" in column 17) must be the name of the record format which exists in the file from which you are stealing the field names.

As you can see from the example in Figure F-13, the format of the keyword is:

FORMAT([library-name/]database-file-name)

The database-file-name parameter is required. It is the name of the physical or logical file from which the previously defined record format is taken. The library-name is optional. If you do not specify the library-name, the library list (*LIBL) in effect at file creation time is used.

Specifying Field Level PF Keywords

Moving down the DDS hierarchy from the record level we find another set of keywords associated with fields. As you are defining physical files, you have a number of valuable keywords to choose from at the field level including: ALIAS, COLHDG, DFT, REFFLD, and of course TEXT.

In Figure F-14, all of these keywords are used to define a Vendor Master Physical File named VNDMSTPF.

Figure F-14 Field Level Physical File Keywords

```
A* PHYSICAL FILE (VNDMSTPF)
A*
A                                   REF(SAMPLE/FIELDREF)
A    R  VNDMSTR                     TEXT('VENDOR DB FORMAT')
        VNDNBR      5  0            COLHDG('VENDOR' 'NUMBER')
                                    ALIAS(VENDOR_NUMBER)
        NAME        R               REFFLD(VNAME VNDMASP)
        ADDR1       25              COLHDG('ADRRESS LINE 1')
        CITY        20              DFT('Wilkes-Barre')
        CODE        1               TEXT('Active Recrd Code')
        ADDR3       R +5            REFFLD(ADDR1 *SRC)
        ... (poor record layout)
```

You may have noticed in the example in Figure F-14 that at the bottom we declared this a poor record layout. Again, this is because we believe that you should use a field reference file or not use a reference file. However, this example gives us a lot to work with.

Working through some of the new stuff, you may have noticed that there are no A's on a number of the statements. This too is OK! Though DDS is supposed to have an A in column six, the syntax checker and the compiler don't really care. They know which checker to use and the checker knows you know there should be an "A" but it does not make you put one in.

COLHDG

Our first new keyword is COLHDG. This is extremely valuable in that it lets you specify the field headings for AS/400 Queries and for screen design prompts, right in the database. When using Query, these column headings will be the default headings for your selected fields. When using SDA, rather than typing the prompt for a field you can just reference database fields and tell them to pop into areas of a panel you are designing. This helps programmer productivity.

When you are typing the column heading keyword, if you want the prompt or report heading to be on one line, after the first parenthesis, you place a quote, then place your prompt, followed by another quote and a closing parenthesis. It would look like the following:

COLHDG('Address Line 1')

If, on the other hand you want your default prompt or report heading to be on two or three lines rather than take up a lot of column width, use the COLHDG keyword in the same fashion, but instead of having just one opening and closing quote, place quotes around each of the up-to three parts of the prompt text. This would look like the following:

COLHDG('VENDOR' 'NUMBER')

ALIAS

The next new keyword is ALIAS. This keyword is used to put a large fieldname into the database. Since RPGIV takes no-larger-than ten characters for field names, we know this is not for RPGIV. However, COBOL likes big moose field names such as:

THE_RETAIL_CATALOG_PRICE

To define these to the database so that both RPG and COBOL can use the field entries, you need both a short and a long of it. The name entry in DDS handles the short fine. The long is implemented in DDS via the ALIAS keyword. If you need a big long field of up to 30 characters, use an ALIAS keyword to get you there.

REFFLD

Use this field-level keyword to refer to a field under one of these three conditions: (1.) When the name of the referenced field is different from the name in positions 19 through 28 (2.) When the name of the referenced field is the same as the name in positions 19 through 28, but the record format, file, or library of the referenced field is different from that specified with the REF keyword. (3.) When the referenced field occurs in the same DDS source file as the referencing field

There are two general formats for this keyword. They are as follows:

Form 1

**REFFLD(record-format-name/
referenced-field-name [blank] library name/file name)**

Form 2

REFFLD(Field name / *SRC)

Example 1

The first example using Form 1 is shown immediately below:

REFFLD(VFORMAT/VNAME VENDLIB/VNDMASP)

Example 2

Using this Form 1, you can also default the record format name as well as the library name giving a statement such as the one we supplied in the source as shown in Figure F-14. This line is repeated below for your convenience:

REFFLD(VNAME VNDMASP)

Using Form 2 of REFFLD

Use *SRC (rather than the database-file-name) when the field name being referred to is in the same DDS source file as the field being defined. *SRC is the default value when the database-file-name and the library-name are not specified. The below example is from the last statement of Figure F-14.

ADDR3 . . . REFFLD(ADDR1 *SRC)

DFT

This field-level keyword is used to specify a default value for a field. In the DDS shown in Figure F-14, there is a default value of the 'Wilkes-Barre' given for CITY. This means that if CITY is not specified in the database for a given record, the default, rather than all blanks, is 'Wilkes-Barre.' This particular entry would come in handy if your business were located in Wilkes-Barre and most of your vendors were from Wilkes-Barre.

There is one more thing to discuss before we can move from Figure F-14. Take another look at the ADDR3 field. You will notice that it has an "R" for reference and it has a REFFLD specified. However, though it wants to use ADDR1 as its reference field, this coding acknowledges that ADDR1 will be too small for this new field ADDR3. The instruction "+5" in the length column tells the DDS compiler to make the ADDR3 field five positions longer in the database than the ADDR1 field. Though not particularly pretty, this is a very powerful facility in DDS.

Specifying Key Field Level PF Keywords

Continuing our road down the DDS specification, we soon find ourselves at the key-field level. In this level, another host of keywords are available. You can use these to direct exactly how the key field or portions of the key field should be used in building the file's index. These keywords are valid for both physical files and logical files. They include the following: DESCEND, ABSVAL, UNSIGNED, SIGNED, DIGIT, ZONE, NOALTSEQ.

ABSVAL

You would use this key field level keyword to direct the OS/400 program to ignore the sign of the field when it sequences the values associated with this numeric field. This keyword has no parameters.

DESCEND

You would use this key field-level keyword to specify that the values of this character, hexadecimal, or numeric key field are retrieved in descending sequence

DIGIT

You would select this key field-level entry to specify that only the digit portion (farthest right 4 bits) of each byte of the key field is used when constructing a value associated with this key field. The zone portion would be zero-filled. Obviously you must have a good reason for doing this. Digit is not one of the frequently used keywords. The keyword has no parameters associated with it. There are some restrictions and caveats, however.

The DIGIT keyword is applied against the entire key field (not just a position within the field). It is valid only for character, hexadecimal, or zoned decimal type fields. You cannot use this keyword with the ABSVAL, SIGNED, or ZONE keywords. If you specify DIGIT for a key field, the value of the field is treated as a string of unsigned binary data, rather than signed data, which is the default for zoned decimal fields. This keyword is the opposite of ZONE

NOALTSEQ

You would use this key field-level keyword to specify that if you first had used the ALTSEQ keyword at the file level, and you do not want it to apply to this key field. If you specify ABSVAL or SIGNED for a key field, then NOALTSEQ is automatically in effect whether or not the NOALTSEQ keyword is specified for that key field.

SIGNED

You would code this key field-level keyword to specify that when sequencing the values associated with this numeric key field, the system is to consider the signs of the values (negative versus positive values)

UNSIGNED

You would use this key field-level keyword to specify that numeric fields are sequenced as a string of unsigned binary data. Character, date, time, timestamp, and hexadecimal fields default to unsigned values when this keyword is supplied.
ZONE

You should use this key field-level keyword to specify that only the zone portion (farthest left 4 bits) of each byte of the key field is to be used when constructing a value associated with this key field. The digit portion is filled with zeros. This keyword is the opposite of DIGIT.

Creating a Physical File

We have mostly exhausted the plethora of keywords that can be employed for physical database files. Before we spice up our days with logical files, let's look again at the process of how to create a physical file once you have determined what your source DDS should look like.

The process involves the following five steps:

1. Invoke PDM to get your productivity list manager going

2. Invoke option 3 of PDM which is SEU (STRSEU)

3. This sets you up so that you can type your DDS specifications into a source file using the Source Entry Utility (SEU). PDM option 3 invokes the SEU editor.

4. Press F6 to add the new member and then entr the DDS source..

5. After the source is entered, then you can use PDM option 14 to compile the source and create the physical database file into a library of your choice

If you were to press the command prompter "F4" after typing in option 14 of PDM, the system would very nicely prompt you for all of the options on the CRTPF command. We have already seen several examples of the CRTPF command. This is yet another one. If you prompted from PDM, the PDM would supply a number of the parameters on the create command for you since PDM knows the source and name information.

A sample of the Create Physical File command you would see after the prompter does its thing is shown in Figure F-15. When you are satisfied that PDM has picked the right options for you, you need only press ENTER and PDM will invoke the DDS compiler, CRTPF, to create a physical file from your DDS.

Figure F-15 Sample Prompted CRTPF Command

```
CRTPF  FILE(*CURLIB/MYFILE) SRCFILE(*LIBL/QDDSSRC) +
SRCMBR(*FILE)  MBR(*FILE)  MAXMBRS(1) +
SIZE(10000 1000 3) DLTPCT(*NONE) TEXT(*SRCMBRTXT)
```

More PF Field Level Keywords

There are a number of physical file field level keywords that can be specified using database DDS but have little or nothing to do with database function. These keywords are also valid for logical files and have the same meaning in both physical and logical files. The COLHDG keyword which we previously covered fits this description. It has value for Screen Design Aid (SDA) development, for DFU and for Query applications. However, it does little for the database. The following keywords fall into the same category as COLHDG: CHECK, COMP, EDTCDE, EDTWRD, RANGE, REFSHIFT, VALUES.

These are most often found in the field reference file when one is deployed. They are not used by the physical file itself. They are data attributes that use the database as a place for their storage. When you link your database to programs or utilities that can extract these attributes, such as display file objects (DSPF) and printer file objects (PRTF), there are productivity and standardization gains achieved. Thus, these attribute keywords should be coded within the database, preferably through a field reference file, since there is no display file or printer file reference file.

If you have no field reference file there is still reason to add these keywords to the database file descriptions. For example, when the database is used as a reference file, all of these display and printer attributes find their way into the display and/or printer files objets merely by having referenced the database file. We show an example of how these keywords are coded in Figure F-19. However, because these keywords pertain to other than database files, there are no detailed explanations of them in this chapter. If you'll pardon me, you can find all the detail you need in IBM's manual sets.

CHECK

You would use this field-level keyword to specify validity checking in display files. CHECK does not affect the physical or logical file being defined. When you define an input-capable field in a display file, refer to the field that you defining in the database by specifying an "R" in position 29 and using the REF or REFFLD keyword. At display file creation, the OS/400 program copies the CHECK keyword and other field attributes from the field in the physical or logical file into the field in the display file.

COMP

You would use this field-level keyword to specify validity checking for the field you are defining if and when it is referred to at a later time during display file creation. You will see later in this book that COMP is also a logical file keyword which is specified at the select/omit-field level. When used in a logical file it is used to control which records are selected to be in the access path or are omitted from the access path. COMP is equivalent to CMP.

EDTCDE and EDTWRD

You would use these field-level keywords to specify editing for the field you are defining when you know the field will be referenced later during display or printer file creation. The EDTCDE and EDTWRD keywords have no effect on the physical or logical file. The physical or logical file merely stores these rules for use in a subsequent program.

The format of the EDTCDE keyword is:

EDTCDE(edit-code)

The format of the EDTWRD keyword is:

EDTWRD('edit-word')

When defining an input-capable field in a display file, you would refer to the field in the database by specifying the letter R in position 29 and the REF or REFFLD keyword. At display file creation, the CRTDSPF command copies the EDTCDE or EDTWRD keyword and other field attributes from the field in the physical or logical file into the field in the display file. RANGE

You would specify this keyword at the field level for a physical or a logical file for validity checking purposes in a display file. For a logical file, the RANGE can also be specified at the select- or omit-field level, or both.

☐ Hint: The RANGE keyword applies to both physical and logical files. In physical files it can be used at the field level only. In logical files, it can be deployed at the field level as well ast the select/omit level.

The format of the RANGE keyword is as follows:

RANGE(low-value high-value)

The following example shows a complete set of complete DDS for a logical file. However, the DDS from statements 20 to 40 are coded the same for a physical file. In this respect, for a physical or a logical file, these statements represent coding being done on behalf of a later to-be-built display file. If the PFILE keyword were removed from the record line (00010) in the sample code below, and line 60 were also removed, this would be all be valid code for using the RANGE keyword with a physical file.

```
00010A R RECORD        PFILE(PF1)
00020A   FIELDA  1 0 RANGE(2 5)
00030A   FIELDB  1   RANGE('2' '5')
00040A   FIELDC
00050A K FIELDB
00060A S FIELDA        RANGE(1 4)
```

In this example, you would code the RANGE (statements 00020 and 00030) as specified for FIELDA and FIELDB for later display file validity checking purposes. At the field level in a physical or logical file, the use of the RANGE is limited as a keyword for display files that later refer to FIELDA and FIELDB. In the display file that would later be built, when this RANGE is in control of a field on a display, it requires that the work station user type only 2, 3, 4, or 5 in FIELDA or FIELDB. FIELDA is an example of coding a numeric field and FIELDB is an example of coding a character field. All of the information in this paragraph pertains to both physical and logical files.

REFSHIFT

The REFSHIFT (Reference Shift) keyword is also valid for both physical and logical files. You would use this field-level keyword to specify that the keyboard should automatically shift for a field when the field is later referred to in a display file or a DFU operation. The format of the keyword is:

REFSHIFT(keyboard-shift)

When you are defining an input-capable field in a display file, you would refer to the REFSHIFT field in the database by specifying the letter R in position 29 and by specifying the REF or the REFFLD keyword. When you create your display file, the CRTDSPF command copies the REFSHIFT keyword and other field attributes from the field in the physical or logical file into the field in the display file.

VALUES

You would specify this keyword at the field level for a physical or a logical file. For a logical file, the VALUES keyword can also be specified at the select- or omit-field level, or both.

☐ Hint: The VALUES keyword applies to both physical and logical files. In physical files it can be used at the field level only. In logical files, it can be deployed at the field level as well ast the select/omit level.

The format of the keyword is:

VALUES(value-1 [value-2...[value-100]])

The following example shows a complete set of complete DDS for a logical file. However, the DDS from statements 20 to 40 are coded the same for a physical file. In this respect, for a physical or a logical file, these statements represent coding being done on behalf of a later to-be-built display file. If the PFILE keyword were removed from the record line (00010) in the sample code below, and lines 50 and 60 were also removed, this would be all be valid code for using the VALUES keyword with a physical file.

```
00010A  R RECORD1    PFILE(PF1)
00020A    FIELDA  1 0 VALUES(1 6 9)
00030A    FIELDB  1  VALUES('A' 'B' 'C')
00040A  K FIELDB
00050A  S FIELDB     VALUES('A' 'B')
00060A  S FIELDA     VALUES(1 6) 2
```

In this example, you would code the VALUES (statements 00020 and 00030) as specified for FIELDA and FIELDB for later display file validity checking purposes. At the field level in a physical or logical file, the use of the VALUES is limited as a keyword for display files that later refer to FIELDA and FIELDB. In the display file that would later be built, when this VALUES keyword is in control of a field on a display, it requires that the work station user type only 1, 6, or 9 in FIELDA or an A, B, or C in FIELDB. FIELDA is an example of coding a numeric field and FIELDB is an example of coding a character field. All of the information in this paragraph pertains to both physical and logical files.

Additional Keywords - Summary

Now, we have examined all of the keywords that you would choose to use in a physical file. Additionally, because certain keywords have two lives and live at different levels and in different file types, we gave you a preview of what life will be like when we cover logical files in the pages ahead. As a last hoorrahh for physical files and as a sendoff for the trusty EARNMAST file, we have taken the liberty of adding a whole collage of these keywords to the EARNMAST DDS as you can well see in Figure F-19.

Figure F-19 Using the Additional PF Keywords

```
A* PHYSICAL FILE (EARNMAST)
A*
A    R  EARNMSTR                    TEXT('Earnings Master')
        EMPNAM     25  0            REFSHIFT(X)
        EMPINL      2               COLHDG('Emp Initials')
        ACCT#       6  0            RANGE(50000000 59999999)
        PAYCOD      1               VALUES('A' 'R' 'D')
        RATE        6  2            COMP(GE 4.65)
                                    EDTCDE(J)
                                    COLHDG('PAY' 'RATE')
        STATUS      1               COLHDG('Pay Status')
        EMPNO       6  0            CHECK(ME MF)
                                    EDTWRD('******')
     ...
```

☐ Hint The DDS in Figure F-19 is built with from / to positions, even though it is not a field reference file. You do not need a field reference file to create a physical file. However, as we have previously noted, all physical database files can be used as field reference files once they are compiled into database objects.

Chapter 10   Coding for Multiple Member Physical Files

Multiple Member Source Files

You have previously noted that a source file can have many different members within the one file. A source file such as QDDSSRC in the HELLO library, for example, would contain as many members as there are different sets of DDS within the file. One source file such as QDDSSRC in HELLO could hold up to 32767 sets of DDS source in 32,767 members. The Create Source Physical File command (CRTSRCPF) defaults to the *NOMAX parameter for number of members. Thus, unless you or somebody else changed your defaults, every one of your source files can contain 32,767 sets of DDS.

Creating a Multi Member Physical File

The Create Physical File command, which can also create a source file, given the proper DDS, expects to be creating normal one member database files. Therefore, IBM set the default maximum members for the CRTPF command to one. In Figure F-15, you can see that this is the value specified in the sample CRTPF command. If you need more than one member, you can change this value when creating your file, or you can use the Change Physical File command (CHGPF)after the file is created. The maximum number of members in a non-source physical file is also 32,767 since a source file is a physical file with a format that accommodates source processing.

From the above discussion you can safely conclude that source files are not the only physical database files which can have multiple members. In fact, any physical file can have more than one member even if it were created with just one member. After file creation, as noted above, using the Change Physical File command (CHGPF) you could adjust the number of members parameter with a specific number or you could set it at *NOMAX for no maximum number limitation.

A physical file with multiple members has a structure which looks like that in Figure F-16.

Figure F-16 Multiple PF Members
Format
R EARNMSTR
EMPNAM   25 0
EMPINL   2
ACCT#   6 0
    ...
Access Path
Member: COMPANY1
Data: Company1
Access Path
Member: COMPANY2
Data: Company2h
Access Path
Member: COMPANY3
Data: Company3

The relevant portions of the three commands which would be necessary to create a three-member physical file are shown in Figure F-17.

Figure F-17 Creating a 3-Member Physical File

```
CRTPF  ...EARNMAST...  MBR(COMPANY1)
MAXMBRS(3)

ADDPFM  FILE(*CURLIB/EARNMAST)
MBR(COMPANY2)

ADDPFM  FILE(*CURLIB/EARNMAST)
MBR(COMPANY3)
```

When the EARNMAST Physical File in Figure F-17 is created, by default the command calls for one member to be created within the file. Using the MBR parameter, the command explicitly names the member COMPANY1. The CRTPF command automatically by default creates one member in each file it creates in addition to creating the file. If you do not specify a member name as we did in Figure F-17, then the compiler will give the one member it creates the same name as the file object which it is creating. You can also use the Rename Member command (RNMM) to rename a member after the fact.

For the two additional members to exist, they must be added to the physical file using the Add Physical File Member ADDPFM command as shown in Figure F-17. Since each of the additional two members use the same format (same fields, keys, record layout etc.), and a physical file can have one and only one format, there is no reason to create a new file for each company. Storing the data in separate members will keep it data separate for record reading and updating but together for full file processing if desired.

Selecting the Member to Process

The Override with Database File command (OVRDBF) typically must be used prior to a program using a multiple member file. If by chance the override is not done, the program will always work with the first member in the file's member list. In the example shown in Figure F-17, therefore, the default is to work with the member named COMPANY1.

If the first member is not the member you want to process, the OVEDBF is needed to select the specific member which will be used. If, the programmer wants to use all members of the file at once, the OVRDBF is again needed. In this case, after the override, data would be presented, one member at a time, until the program finishes. If the file had a key, for example, the records in the members would not be merged into key order before being presented. The first member would be processed, followed by the second, followed by the third. The overrides for processing all three members at once would look as follows:

OVRDBF FILE(EARNMAST) MBR(*ALL)

Likewise, the CL override necessary to process only the second member would be as follows:

OVRDBF FILE(EARNMAST) MBR(COMPANY2)

And, to process just the third member of the EARNMAST Physical file, you would use the following CL override:

OVRDBF FILE(EARNMAST) MBR(COMPANY3)

How do you get data into your new EARNMAST file? The answer is the same way you would get data into any other physical file. You could use the IBM Data File Utility program (DFU), or you could write a file maintenance program since EARNMAST is a master file. If the file were a transaction file, the transaction processing program such as Order Entry would provide the data as a natural part of its operation.

The fact that EARNMAST has three separate and distinct members, one for each separate company, means that the file must be overridden to select the proper member prior to running any program. Developers will typically create a CL program which performs the override to the specific file and then calls the program to process the file. The program has no clue as to which member it is actually using. The override alerts the database and that's all that is necessary.

Populating the File - Summary

In summary then, once you have your file and member picked and properly selected with an override, then you have a few choices as to how to populate the file:

1. An interactive Data Entry Program
2. A batch program (can select data to add to the new file)
3. The Data File Utility (DFU) or SQL
4. The Copy Utility
5. Other

In the next chapter we examine one of the most powerful utilities on the system. It is typically the ideal tool for populating database files when the data is available in another form such as a spreadsheet or a PC file.

Chapter 11   Copy Utility for Populating Physical Files

A Powerful Tool

The Copy File Utility is an extremely powerful tool on the AS/400. It provides enough value to AS/400 programmers that it certainly has earned its spot in this book. The best way to learn the Copy File utility is to engage it for action. Take it for a ride. Type in COPY on a command line and press F4 to get all of the prompts. When a prompt is not self-explanatory, position your cursor to the prompt line and press F1 or the Help key, to get a more complete explanation. The AS/400 Help text is very good. In the example in Figure F-18, we cover some of the more popular options and capabilities of the Copy Utility (Command).

Figure F-18A COPY Utility Command

```
CPYF
FROMFILE(HELLO/OLDEARN)
TOFILE(HELLO/EARNMAST)
MBROPT(*ADD)                    *REPLACE
FMTOPT(*MAP)          *DROP  |  *NOCHK
CRTFILE(*NO)                      *YES
```

Renaming EARNMAST

Assume, for the example in Figure F-18A, that OLDEARN is a prior EARNMAST file. In Figure F-17, you have already created a new EARNMAST physical file. To make the example more believable, let us assume that you have added a new field to the new EARNMAST file. The file is empty. It contains no records. The prior records, without the new field, are stored in a file called OLDEARN. Let us also assume that OLDEARN was created by renaming the EARNMAST file to OLDEARN using the following command:

RNMOBJ OBJ(HELLO/EARNMAST) OBJTYPE(*FILE) NEWOBJ(OLDEARN)

This is a common technique used to save the data from a file when field lengths are being changed or fields are being added or deleted to a file. After the rename, EARNMAST is no longer on the system, but all of its attributes and data are preserved in the OLDEARN file in the HELLO library.

CPYF

The objective of the CPYF command, then, is to populate our new file, EARNMAST with the data from OLDEARN. The CPYF program in Figure F-18A would take the old EARNMAST records currently stored in the OLDEARN file and would copy them to the new earnings master file (EARNMAST).

CPYF Replace or Add

But, CPYF wants a few questions answered before it does its job for you. For example, do you want the new records that are copied, to replace any old records, which might already be there? This is the *REPLACE option. Do you want to add the new records to any existing records that may already be there? This is the *ADD option. For this example, either option will work since there are no records in the newly created EARNMAST file. For this CPYF, we selected the *ADD option.

One more point before doing the copy. The override from above is set to use the member named COMPANY3 which was created in the example shown in Figure F-17. Member COMPANY3 is used because it was our last override above. Unmodified overrides last until you sign off your device.

CPYF *MAP and *DROP

CPYF also has some other very important questions it must have answered in order to copy correctly: Does the data that is in the from-file have the same shape or format as the data in the to-file? In this example, we added a new field to the new EARNMAST file. This makes it a different shape from the OLDEARN file. We did not change the length or remove a field from the new file, but since we added a new field (assume in the middle of the record) the from-file and the to-file no longer have the same shape,

The CPYF program is smart. It is aware that it is working with an integrated database system. As such, it gives utility far beyond what any other system can provide. In this example, as shown in Figure F-18A, you would pick the format option *MAP so that the CPYF program can properly take the from-fields of the OLDEARN file and direct their data into the to-fields of the same name in the EARNMAST file. It would do this mapping as directed even if the new fields were bigger.

If you removed a field from DDS before the CRTPF command, you would pick the *DROP option in addition to *MAP so that the CPYF program would drop any fields from the old file which were not defined in the new file.

Copy File and Flat Files

In addition to helping you map your old data to new data, the CPYF program can also take data from databases and copy it to the equivalent of flat files. It can also take a flat file and bring it right into a database file using the *NOCHK option. In both of these cases, the flat file record layout must correspond 100% to the layout of the database file. Let's take an example. Suppose on a Unix box, we had a file with three fields – such as:

Name   **30 positions**
Address   **30 Positions**
City   **20 Positions**

☐ Hint: It would be helpful for you to have an appreciation for Tape, CD, and DVD data management, as well as PDM, and SEU to achieve the five tasks below. The data management knowledge can be gained by working with AS/400 commands such as CPYFRMTAP and absorbing the help text. It can also be gained by reading IBM's web based documentation. We show you how to find IBM manuals in the Appendix of this book. For PDM and SEU, you can again use IBM's Web documentation library or you can use the IBM i Pocket Developers' Guide to help you earn all you need to know about SEU and PDM.

It is clear that the record length, if we add the lengths of the three fields together, is 80 positions. The data from the Unix box can be brought to the AS/400 in a standard fixed record length tape or CD or DVD from the Unix box. To store the data on the AS/400 and move it into a database file, you would perform the following five steps:

1.   Create an AS/400 file called UNIXDATA in the HELLO library with a record length of 80. You would need no DDS. The CRTPF command would create a file with a one big field named UNIXDATA, the same as the file name. The command would look as follows:

CRTPF FILE(HELLO/UNIXDATA) RCDLEN(80)

2.   You would then use Client Access or FTP or even the Copy From Tape command (CPYFRMTAP) to get the data into the AS/400 disk file. Whichever option we choose to bring data in, after the commands are executed, the Unix data sits in the UNIXDATA file in the HELLO library. Though a full description of tape processing options is beyond this book, we show a sample CPYFRMTAP below to help complete the example:

**CPYFRMTAP FROMFILE(QTAPE)
TOFILE(HELLO/UNIXDATA) FROMDEV(TAP01)
FROMRCDLEN(80) FROMENDOPT(*REWIND)
MBROPT(*REPLACE) FROMBLKLEN(8000)
FROMRCDBLK(*FB)**

3.   You would then use PDM and SEU to build DDS to reflect the fields: Name, Address, and City. You would then create a file called NAFILE using PDM option 14, referencing the DDS you just created. The DDS would look similar to those in Figure F-18B:

Figure F-18B DDS for Flat File Conversion

```
Columns . . . :    1  71              Edit              HELLO/QDDSSRC
SEU==>                                                           NAFILE
FMT A*  .....A*. 1 ...+... 2 ...+... 3 ...+... 4 ...+... 5 ...+... 6 ...+... 7
        *************** Beginning of data ************************************
0001.00     A*                                    ('NAFILE DB FILE')
0002.00     A          R NARF                     TEXT('NAME OF DB RECORD FOR
0003.00     A            NAME          30         COLHDG('NAME')
0004.00     A                                     TEXT('NAME FIELD')
0005.00     A            ADDRES        30         COLHDG('ADDRESS')
0006.00     A                                     ALIAS(ADDRESS)
0007.00     A            CITY          20         COLHDG('ADDRESS')
0008.00     A                                     TEXT('CONTAINS HW TRANSLATI
0009.00     A* BELOW REPEAT OF NAME FIELD IS TO DEFINE IT AS THE KEY TO FILE
0010.00     A          K NAME
        ***************** End of data ******************************************




   F3=Exit   F4=Prompt   F5=Refresh  F9=Retrieve  F10=Cursor  F11=Toggle
   F16=Repeat find       F17=Repeat change       F24=More keys
                               (C) COPYRIGHT IBM CORP. 1981, 2000.
```

4.   You would then invoke the CPYF utility as shown below and you would specify *NOCHK for the FMTOPT parameter. The CPYF program would then take the big 80-byte field named UNIXDATA, from the UNIXDATA flat file and plunk it byte for byte into an 80-byte record chopped up into three fields in the NAFILE format called NARF.

.   The command would not check to assure that fields lined up since you told it not to check by specifying *NOCHK. The 80-byte field does not map size-wise into any of the three database fields. Moreover, there is no equivalently named field in the To-File in which the 80-byte field named UNIXDATA can be received. There is no sense telling the CPYF utility to check the data since any check on the data would stop the copy. With *NOCHK, you are on your own. It is up to your own editing to assure that the data lines up when the CPYF is complete.

.   The data from 1 to 30 in the UNIXDATA field would naturally arrive in the NAME filed, from 31 to 60 would arrive in the ADDRES field, and the data from 61 to 80 would arrive in the CITY field. Because the *NOCHK option in essence instructs the COPY command to overlay all three fields with the record information, as long as the data is lined up properly in the from-record, it will be fine in the to-record. The command to perform this is given below:

CPYF FROMFILE(HELLO/UNIXDATA) TOFILE(HELLO/NAFILE) MBROPT(*REPLACE) FMTOPT(*NOCHK)

5.   Because most successful, detail-oriented, IT folks are skeptics at heart, you would then take option 18 from PDM Work With Objects (DFU) to see that the data arrived properly. You might also issue a STRQRY command and build a simple query to get a report on the new data. For the bit-heads among us, why format? Just use the IBM command, Display Physical File Member (DSPPFM) and you can see the

hex representation of the file so that even the slightest detail can be checked. The PDM option 18 and the DSPPFM command are shown immediately below:

18 NAFILE PF   N/A File For Unix Data

DSPPFM FILE(HELLO/NAFILE)

Chapter 12   Introduction to Logical File Coding - DDS Levels

Introduction

Well, we did it! We covered physical database file coding and creation, multiple member files, and the great data populater, the CPYF utility. Now, we turn our attention to logical files – the function which may very well be the reason for a relational database in the first place. One thing is for sure, we covered the topics in the correct sequence since, try as you may, you cannot create a logical file without there first being a physical file upon which to base your logical file.

In the next part of this book, we will introduce various topics pertaining to logical file including detailed explanations of important keywords and coding examples for both single & multiple format logical files and we will be using the relational database operators which we described earlier. As you may recall, these are: Union, Projection, Selection, and Join – as well as Order. We will also review access path sharing (Chapter 6 - under heading Sharing Access Paths) and format sharing (Chapter 9, under heading FORMAT). We will also provide examples and a detailed description of logical file selections using select/omit logic. There are examples which use both immediate selection and dynamic selection (DYNSLT).

Logical Files Make Sense

If we can think of a logical file simply as a means of providing how data records are selected and transformed when read by an application or utility program, these examples will make more sense. They will also make more sense, sooner. Eventually, I would expect them to all make sense to you.

Non-Join Logical Files

There are two different types of logical files. The first type is the more simple which we refer to as non-join logical files. These can be very simple, such as when they are based upon just one physical file. However, they can become more complex. For example, a non-join, single format logical file — also referred to as a UNION may be built over as many as 32 physical files. All files would have the same format in this case. Additionally, a non-join, multiple format logical file can also be based on as many as 32 physical files, and up to 32 different formats from the underlying physical files.

Join Logical Files

If we begin with the types of non-join logical files we can have, if you'll pardon the pun, it is "logical" that the next type of logical file to discuss is the join logical file. The join logical file is more complex. It introduces a number of different DDS keywords which do not play in the non-join arena. However, for the additional complexity, it provides necessary facility to any relational database and we believe is one of the most valuable capabilities provided by a relational database.

With the notion of the join logical file, it again helps to remember that all data flows from physical files and that the type of logical file deployed is controlled by DDS keywords. There is no data in a join logical file. Just like all other logical files, it provides a set of rules that make the data appear to be coming from a single format physical file, but the reality is that all data is retrieved from the underlying physical files when using any logical view.

The chart in Figure F-20 summarizes what we have just discussed and shows the specifics of both the join and non-join types of files.

Figure F-20 Types of Logical Files

Non-join	Join		
1 PF	2-32 PFs	DFTVAL	No default
	1 Format		
	Outer Join	Inner Join	
(Union)	2-32 Formats		

Six Levels of DDS

Though not all types of entries are required in all cases, non-join logical files use five of the six levels of DDS entries as follows:

1. **File-Level Entries**
2. **Record-Level Entries**
3. **Join Record-Level Entries**
4. **Field-Level Entries**
5. **Key Field-Level Entries**
6. **Select/Omit-Level Entries**

Non-Join Logical Files- Coding

We will examine all six levels of logical file DDS coding. But, we will save the JOIN File description until we have discussed all other levels. Since the JOIN specifications typically use most of the other levels, you will be in a better position to appreciate the nuances of the join after you have most of the other information under your belt.

Our approach in this section will be to describe what happens in each of the levels of DDS and how you code to make things happen. To do this, we will closely examine the most popular DDS keywords (and some not so popular) so that when we hit the full DDS examples, you will be better prepared to understand their underpinnings.

Many of the keywords we are examining have already been fully explained In Chapter 9 since they also pertain to physical files. Where it is better to repeat information, we will do so, but we will also refer you back to Chapter 9 as appropriate.

Let's start our logical file level adventure with the Big Cohuna of all levels - the File Level.

File Level Keywords

Application requirements are the determining factor as to which levels and which keywords should be used in a given project. The file level keywords used in non-join logical files include the following:

DYNSLT   Select records only when view is used

ALTSEQ   Use different collating sequence

FCFO   Use first-changed, first-out sequencing of
           duplicate keys

FIFO   Use first-in, first-out sequencing of duplicate keys

UNIQUE   No duplicate keys allowed

LIFO   Use last-in, first-out sequencing of duplicate keys

DYNSLT is the only new keyword in the list above. The other five keywords are described in detail in Chapter 9 as physical file "file- level" entries. Because these four keywords control the sequencing of keyed records, they pertain to keyed physical files as well as logical files. As such, they received full treatment in Chapter 9. DYNSLT is covered in detail in Chapter 15.

Record Level Keywords

PFILE--Specify based on physical file name and library (optional) for logical file

FORMAT--Share the format of another file - also involved to perform equivalent of a rename format

TEXT--Provides textual documentation at the record level

Field Level Keywords

ALIAS--Provides another name for a field. Most valuable for giving fields longer names for use in COBOL programs.

CONCAT--Use for concatenation of fields - such as making a date field from Month, Day and Year fields.

FLTPCN--Use the FLTPCN keyword to specify double precision or to change the precision of an already specified floating-point field.

RENAME--Use to rename a physical file field for use in a logical file

SST--Use for sub-stringing fields – such as taking a date field and creating a month field. It is the opposite of CONCAT.

TRNTBL--Provides a table to translate the data from a field that is read from a physical file through a logical field

Because they are so important and so common to logical files, before we move on to more logical file keywords, key field keywords, and select/omit keywords, we will take a deeper look at the CONCAT, RENAME and SST field level keywords.

CONCAT

The Concatenate keyword (CONCAT) is available for use in logical files only. You would put this field-level keyword to use when you want to combine two or more fields from a physical file record format into one field in the logical file record format you are defining.

The first necessary component of a CONCAT operation is that the name of the new, concatenated field must appear in positions 19 through 28 of the DDS specification. The second component is the CONCAT keyword which is specified in the functions area (column 45) as are all DDS keywords. of CONCAT keyword

The format of the keyword is:

CONCAT(field-1 field-2 . . .)

You would specify the physical file field names in the order in which you want them to be concatenated. The fields must be separated by one or more blanks, and separate them by blanks.

☐ Hint: If you specify the same physical field more than once in a record format in the logical file — by using either RENAME or CONCAT, the top-to-bottom sequence in which you specify the fields in the logical file is the sequence in which the data is moved to the physical file on an update or insert operation.

Within your program, each field in the logical file would have its own storage. When your program updates through a logical view in which CONCATs and /or RENAMEs are used, data management actually updates the underlying physical record just once. Therefore, as it builds the physical record to be written or updated, it moves the data to the physical file one logical field at a time. Thus, the value in the last occurrence of the physical field is the value that is put in the physical record and is the value that is used for all keys built over that physical field. All previous values of the same physical field are overlayed by the final value. The net effect is that they are ignored.

The following examples show how you specify the CONCAT keyword in DDS

Example 1

In this example, there are three fields - FIRST, SECOND, and THIRD involved in the concatenation. All of these fields in the physical file are to be concatenated into one field called THREE in the logical file, as shown in the following example.

```
00010A   R RCD1R   PFILE(PF1)
00020A     THREE   CONCAT(FIRST SECOND THIRD)
```

Example 2

In the following, if the program changes THREE from AA BB CC to XX YY ZZ, the value placed in the physical record does not change because the fields specified last are FIRST (value AA), SECOND(value BB), and THIRD (value CC). However, if FIRST, SECOND, and THIRD are changed to new values in a program, the values in the physical record also changed.

```
00010A R RCD2R   PFILE(PF1)
00020A THREE   CONCAT(FIRST SECOND THIRD)
00030A FIRST
00040A SECOND
00050A THIRD
```

Example 3

In the following example, fields from the physical file are concatenated into more than one field in the logical file.

```
00010A R RCD3R   PFILE(PF1)
00020A  FISETH   CONCAT(FIRST SECOND THIRD)
00030A  THFISE   CONCAT(THIRD FIRST SECOND)
```

Example 4

There is a ton of rules for determining whether a result field is a variable length field or a fixed length field when two unlike fields are concatenated. You could check these rules if you like, by perusing the IBM Physical and Logical File DDS guide in the IBM Web Documentation. Rather than put you through the pain of reading all the rules and wondering what they are all about, we present the following example in which the fields from the physical file have the following names and types:

FIXEDA	**Fixed length field.**
FIXEDB	**Fixed length field.**
VARLENA	**Variable length field.**

There are three concatenations coded below in the DDS. The first (00020) takes an undefined field (in terms of variable length or fixed length) called FIELDA, and gives it a value of the concatenation of a fixed length field. Because a variable length field was involved in the concatenation, FIELDA becomes a variable length field. The second (00030) concatenation takes two fixed length fields and FIELD B winds up as a fixed length field because the two concatenated fields are fixed length. In the third DDS CONCAT (00040) FIELDC is defined as variable length in this set of DDS. Even though the concatenation is of two fixed length fields, because FIELDC is defined as variable length, the result of the CONCAT is a variable length field.

In summary, the resulting fields that would be presented to a HLL program are as follows:

FIELDA	**Variable length field**
FIELDB	**Fixed length field**
FIELDC	**Variable length field**

The Code

```
00010A   R RCD4R        PFILE(PF1)
00020A     FIELDA       CONCAT(FIXEDA VARLENA)
00030A     FIELDB       CONCAT(FIXEDA FIXEDB)
00040A     FIELDC       CONCAT(FIXEDA FIXEDB)
00050A                  VARLEN
```

RENAME

The Rename Field keyword (RENAME) is available for use in logical files only. You would put this field-level keyword to use when you want to rename a fields from a physical file record format in the logical file record format you are defining. You would use this keyword when you want a field name in the logical record format you are defining to be different from its corresponding physical file field name.

The format of the RENAME keyword is:

RENAME(physical-file-field-name)

The name as it appears in the physical file record format is the one parameter value for this keyword. One particular field in the physical file record format can be renamed multiple times in a logical file format. There are a number of reasons why you might want to rename a field through a logical view:

1. You want to use programs that were written using a different name for the same field.

2. You want to map one field in a physical file record format to two or more fields in a logical file record format.

3. You are using a high-level language that does not permit two fields having different names to have only one data storage area. By specifying the RENAME keyword, you allow both fields to access the same data storage area.

Just as with the CONCAT statement which we described above, the top-to-bottom sequencing of multiple renames of the same physical field determines what data actually gets written during a WRITE or UPDATE operation in an HLL program.

The following examples show how to specify the RENAME keyword.

Example 1

In the example immediately below, the OLDFIELD field in the physical file (PF1) is renamed NEWNAME in the logical file.

```
00010A R RCD1R          PFILE (PF1)
00020A   NEWNAME         RENAME (OLDFIELD)
```

Example 2

In the following example, the renamed field in the logical file (NEWNAME) is used as a key field.

```
00010A R RCD1R          PFILE (PF1)
00020A   NEWNAME         RENAME (OLDFIELD)
00030A K NEWNAME
```

SST

The Substring keyword (SST) is available for use in logical files only. You would put this field-level keyword to use when you want to use a piece of a field value from a physical file record format in the logical file record format you are defining. You would use this keyword to specify a character string that is a subset of an existing character, hexadecimal, zoned field, or graphic field.

The format of the keyword is:

SST(field-name starting-position [length])

The first parameter you specify in the SST operation is the fieldname. This specifies the name of the field from which the substring is taken. The field must be defined in the same logical file format prior to the SST field (which is the field you are defining) or it must exist in the physical file specified on a PFILE or JFILE keyword (JFILE is a Join record level keyword).

□ Note: Though we do not like to spend the time and space for rules in an action-oriented, example driven book, simply because rules are boring. If you are reading the rules below and you get a bit bored, consider this small section reference material and move on!

The rules for SST are reasonable and relatively easy to comprehend. To find the field, the database searches for a matching field name using the following rules:

1. First, the database searches the field names specified in positions 19 to 28 in the logical file format prior to the SST field.

2. If it finds no matching field name in positions 19 to 28 in the logical file format, the database searches for the field name in the physical file as specified on the PFILE or JFILE keyword, using another set of rules as follows:

A. If the logical file is a simple or multiple format logical file, the field must exist in all files specified on the PFILE keyword.

B. If the logical file is a join logical file and the JREF keyword is specified on the SST field, the field must exist in the JFILE referred to by the JREF keyword.

C. If the logical file is a join logical file and the JREF keyword is not specified on the SST field, the field must exist in exactly one JFILE.

The second parameter you specify in the SST operation is the starting character position of the string within the field specified in the first parameter. The substring thus begins at the starting position you specify on the SST keyword.

The third parameter (optional) you specify in the SST operation is the length of the string which you are taking from the starting position, defined in the second parameter, of the field whose name you specify in the first parameter of the SST operation. Thus you specify the name of the field which has the string, the starting position of the sub string, and how many characters you want to be part of the new substring field which references the substring.

As another option for the length parameter, you can also specify the substring length on the field length column (DDS positions 30 through 34). As you would expect, the name and starting position are required parameters; the length is optional.

Example 1

The following example shows how to specify the SST keyword on a simple or a multiple format logical file.

```
A R RCD1R            PFILE(PF1)
A   FIRSTNAME I      SST(EMPNAM 1 10)
A K LASTNAME
```

In this example, the FIRSTNAME field is a substring of EMPNAM from PF1. The substring begins in position 1 of EMPNAM and continues to position 10. The usage (I in position 38 of DDS) must be specified for SST fields in simple or multiple format logical files.

Example 2

The following example shows how to specify the SST keyword on a simple logical file.

```
A R RCDR2            PFILE(PF1)
A   ADDR1
A   STATE      I     SST(ADDR1 44 2)
A   CYR        I     SST(CREATEDATE 5)
A   VNAME
A   VENDNAME   I     SST(VNAME 11 10)
A K CYR
```

This example shows:

1. STATE is a substring of ADDR1 from the logical format It starts in position 44 for a length of 2.

2. CYR is a substring of CREATEDATE and is built to hold the year the record was created. It starts in position 5 for a length of 2 (end of field)

3. VENDNAME is a substring of VNAME. It starts in position 11 for a length of 10.

4. Since CYR is a key field, the unique field name CREATEDATE must exist in PF1.

5. The usage (position 38) for a field with the SST keyword must be I (input only).

Example 3

The following example shows how to specify the SST keyword on a join logical file. You may want to make a note of this page and come back later after we cover Join logical files.

```
A R RCDR1            JFILE (PF1 PF2)
A J                  JOIN (1 2)
A                    JFLD (STATE STATE)
A   ADDR1            JREF (2)
A   STATE       I    SST (ADDR1 44 2)
A                    JREF (2)
A   CYR         I    SST (CREATEDATE 5)
A   VNAME            JREF (1)
A   VENDNAME    I    SST (VNAME 11 10)
A                    JREF (2)
A K CYR
```

This example shows:

1. STATE is a substring of ADDR1 from the logical format and PF2, and is joined with STATE from PF1. It starts in position 44 for a length of 2.

2. CYR is a substring of CREATEDATE and is built to
    hold the year the record was created. It starts in position
    five for a length of 2 (end of field)

3. VENDNAME is a substring of VNAME from PF2,
    since VNAME in the logical file format has a different
    JREF. It starts in position 11 for a length of 10.

4. Since CYR is a key field, the unique field name
    CREATEDATE must exist in PF1, not PF2.

5. The usage (position 38) for a field with the SST keyword
    must be I (input only). Since this is a join logical file, the
    usage default is always I.

More LF Field Level Keywords

The following keywords are not used for logical files per se but
provide information to display files and other programs used on
the AS/400 and IBM i. These keywords have previously been
discussed in Chapter 9 under the heading More PF Field Level
Keywords.

CHECK
COMP
COLHDG
EDTCDE
EDTWRD
RANGE
REFSHIFT
TEXT
VALUES

Logical File Key-Field Level Keywords

The use of the logical file Key-Field level keywords is exactly the same as for physical file definitions. The detailed explanations of the following keywords which are used at the Key-Field level for logical views are provided in Chapter 9 under the heading: Specifying Key-Field Level PF Keywords.

DESCEND
ABSVAL
UNSIGNED
SIGNED
DIGIT
ZONE
NOALTSEQ

Logical File Select/Omit Level Keywords

COMP   Use with an S or O in position 17 to provide comparison values for select/omit processing. Use to select or omit fields with a specific code.

RANGE   Use with an S or O in position 17 to provide a range of values for record selection or omission in select/omit processing

VALUES   Use with an S or O in position 17 to provide a list of values to be selected or omitted in select/omit processing

ALL   Use ALL with S in position 17 to tell the database to select any records that do not meet any of the other select/omit rules specified above the ALL. Specify O to omit any records that do not meet any of the other select/omit rules.

Detailed Look at Select /Omit Keywords

Logical File selection is provided by the combination of the S and O codes in column 17 and the four logical file selection keywords examined in general terms above.

☐ Note: Because this is such an important topical area in the study of logical files, we are providing a detailed explanation and specific examples for each of the select/omit keywords. This is provided in addition to all of the specific DDS how-to examples and their associated descriptions.

Additionally, in the detailed description of the COMP keyword below, we have included a section called Select/Omit Rules. Rather than describe these rules in this general area, prior to discussing the keywords and examples, we placed these rules within an example context and use the code in the COMP section to demonstrate the rules.

The following detailed explanations of select / omit keywords also include specific select / omit examples for your edification.

ALL

Because we like to start simple, and because we are covering these logical file select/omit keywords in alphabetical sequence, we shall cover the ALL keyword first. You use this select/omit field-level keyword to specify the action to be taken after all other select/omit specifications have been processed for the logical file.

Works With "O" and "S"

Just as all select specifications, you would specify ALL with an S in position 17 when you want any records that do not meet any of the other select/omit rules (preceding the ALL) to be selected. Selected in this instance means to be included in the view verses omitted or excluded from the view. You would specify the ALL keyword with an O in position 17 to omit any records that do not meet any of the other select/omit rules.

It follows that when you specify the ALL keyword, it must follow all of the other select/omit statements. It is the leftover clause. You do not specify a field name with the ALL keyword. It does not make sense and the DDS compiler does not let you do it.

This ALL keyword has no parameters. It is therefore very easy to coded.

Life Without "ALL"

It is just as important that you understand what happens when you do not specify ALL and you have used select / omit logic. Say you have five OR specifications which are all S in 17 - select oriented. If the record does not match any of the five COMP operations, and it falls through to the end of the select/omit specs, does it get selected? That is the question. The answer in this case is No! Why? Because we were specifically selecting records, the default is to omit if ALL is not specified.

Now, say you have five OR specifications which are all O in 17 - omit oriented. If the record does not match any of the five COMP operations, and it falls through to the end of the select/omit specs, does it get selected? That is the question. The answer in this case is YES! Why? Because we were specifically omitting records, the default is to select the others if ALL is not specified

What happens if there are S records and O records (column 17)? If you do not specify the ALL keyword, the default action taken is the exact opposite of the last select/omit statement in the DDS. Thus, if the last statement was a select, the default is to omit all. If the last statement was an omit, the default is to select all. It does not matter how many O's or S's came before the last statement!

"ALL" Code Snippet

Let's look at an example DDS snippet, which shows how to specify the ALL keyword in your logical file DDS.

```
00010A   S ACT   COMP(EQ 3000)
00020A   S ACT   COMP(GT 3100)
00030A   O AMT   COMP(LT 0)
00040A   O               ALL
```

Suffice it to say that if none of the S's or O's match the record, then the default for the record is to be omitted.

COMP

When used in a logical file it controls which records are selected to be in the access path or are omitted from the access path.

The word COMP is short for comparison and that is its function. It is valid in physical and logical files at the field level. At the field level, it is used for display file and other validity checking. But, its key use for logical files is in the select/omit level where it controls which records are included in a view and which records are not included.

COMP Function and Forms

COMP is equivalent to the CMP keyword, which has been around for twenty-years. COMP is now the preferred keyword. You would use this select/omit level logical file keyword, to select records or omit records, based on specific values in specific fields which you test. At the select omit level, you specify an S in column 17 for selection and you specify an O for omission.

The formats of the keyword are as follow:

COMP(relational-operator value)

COMP(relational-operator field-name)

COMP Relational Operators

With the relational operator, you specify the type of selection or omission you require. You test for equal, greater than, less than, etc. On the other side of the relational operator, you specify the filed name or the value which you are specifically testing.

The valid relational operators are as follows:

Operator	Meaning
EQ	Equal to
NE	Not equal to
LT	Less than
NL	Not less than
GT	Greater than
NG	Not greater than
LE	Less than or equal to
GE	Greater than or equal to

You can specify the value parameter at either the field level or the select/omit field level. However, a field name can be supplied only at the select/omit field level in a logical file. Here are a few examples showing the power of the COMP operation at the select / omit level and the field level.

Example A:

```
00010A  R RECORD    PFILE(PF1)
00020A
00030A    FIELDA    COMP(NE 0)
C0040A    FIELDB    COMP(NE 'A')
00050A    FIELDC
00060A    FIELDD
00070A    FIELDX
00080A  K FIELDB
00090A  S FIELDC    COMP(EQ FIELDX)
00100A  S FIELDA    COMP(NE 0) 2
00110A  S FIELDD    COMP(NE *NULL)
00120A  O FIELDB    COMP(GE 'A')
```

At statements 00020 and 00030, the COMP keyword is specified for both FIELDA and FIELDB as a validity checking keyword for any display files that may reference FIELDA and / or FIELDB.

At statements 90 through 120, the COMP keyword is specified as a select/omit keyword for FIELDC, FIELDA, FIELDD, and FIELDB. When processing through this view, records from the physical file PF1 are retrieved depending on the result of the following comparisons:

1. FIELDC: Records are always selected when FIELDC equals FIELDX.

2. FIELDA: Records not meeting the FIELDC test are tested at this statement. They are selected using this S COMP statement only when FIELDA is not equal to zero.

3. FIELDD: Records not meeting FIELDA test or the FIELDC test are tested at this statement. They are selected only when FIELDD is not a null value.

4. FIELDB Those records not selected in the above three tests are tested. They are specifically omitted if FIELDB is greater than or equal to the letter "A."

Select/Omit Rules

There are some rules to remember when both select and omit keywords:

1. All select/omit level compares are OR conditions when the S or O designation is specifically entered in column 17. When column 17 is blank, after the first S or O specification, the blank COMP records are logically ANDed with the above O or S specification. There are no ANDed specifications in the example above. All are ORs. In an OR condition, whenever a comparison is satisfied, the record is selected or omitted, no other comparisons are made for the record, and the next record is processed.

2. If you specify both select and omit for a record format, the order in which you specify the keywords, is very important. The statements are processed in the order in which they are specified. Thus, if a record satisfies an early statement, the record is either selected or omitted as specified, and any remaining select/omit statements are not examined for that record. In other words, once the criteria for selection or omission is met, the record is selected. No other selection tests are required. The record is either specifically selected or omitted and the next record is processed.

3. If you specify both select and omit statements, you can indicate whether records not meeting any of the values specified are to be selected or omitted. You do this by specifying the ALL keyword on the last select/omit statement. If you specify S, the records not meeting the comparisons are selected. If you specify O, the records not meeting a specific comparison are omitted.

4. If you do not specify the ALL keyword, as in the example above, the action taken for the records that do not meet the values is the converse of the type of the last statement specified. Records that do not meet selection values are omitted, and records that do not meet omission values are selected. In the example above, all records not meeting any of the values would be selected since the last operation is an OMIT (O in 17).

Here is another example:

Example B:

This example specifies the COMP keyword using a hexadecimal character string.

```
00010A   R RCD1      PFILE(PF1)
00020A     FIELDA
00030A     FIELD1
00040A     FIELD2
00050A   K FIELD1
00060A   S FIELDA    COMP(EQ X'51')
00070A     FIELD1    COMP(NE X' ')
```

In this example, the COMP keyword is specified as a select/omit keyword for FIELDA (which is defined as a 1-byte field in the physical file). Records from physical file PF1 are retrieved through this record format only if the value of field CODEA is equal to a hex 51 and if the value of FIELD1 is not blank.

RANGE

You would specify this keyword at the field level for a physical or a logical file. For a logical file, the RANGE can also be specified at the select- or omit-field level, or both.

☐ Hint: The RANGE keyword also applies to physical files and logical files when specified at the field level for validity checking in display files.

RANGE Function and Form

The RANGE keyword is used in the select/omit level with either a select (S) or Omit (O) option specified in column 17. It works very similarly to the COMP operation. However, instead of one value being tested a range of values is tested. The select/omit rules described under COMP also apply to RANGE.

The format of the keyword is:

RANGE(low-value high-value)

RANGE Example

The following example shows a complete set of complete DDS for a logical file. However, the DDS from statements 00020 to 00040 are coded the same for a physical file when specifying a validity check for a display file. In this respect, for a physical or a logical file, these statements represent coding being done on behalf of a later to-be-built display file. If the PFILE keyword were removed from the record line (00010) in the sample code below, and line 00060 were also removed, this would be all be valid code for using the RANGE keyword with a physical file.

```
00010A     R RECORD        PFILE(PF1)
00020A       FIELDA    1 0 RANGE(2 5)
00030A       FIELDB    1   RANGE('2' '5')
00040A       FIELDC
00050A     K FIELDB
00060A     S FIELDA        RANGE(1 4)
```

RANGE at the Field Level

In this example, you would code the RANGE (statements 00020 and 00030) as specified for FIELDA and FIELDB for later display file validity checking purposes. At the field level in a physical or logical file, the use of the RANGE is limited as a keyword for display files that later refer to FIELDA and FIELDB. In the display file that would later be built, when this RANGE is in control of a field on a display, it requires that the work station user type only 2, 3, 4, or 5 in FIELDA or FIELDB. FIELDA is an example of coding a numeric field and FIELDB is an example of coding a character field. All of the information in this paragraph pertains to both physical and logical files.

RANGE at the Select/Omit Level

For logical files only: You would also code the RANGE at statement 00060, if you were using that range for selecting or omitting records via a logical file. It is not at first obvious that statements 00020 and 00060 above are not mutually exclusive. They mean different things. As you can see in this example, on statement 00060, the RANGE is specified as a select/omit keyword for FIELDA. Records from the physical file PF1 are retrieved through this logical file record format only if the value of FIELDA is 1, 2, 3, or 4. The RANGE on statement 00020 is for later use in a display file for validity checking.

VALUES

You would specify this keyword at the field level for a physical or a logical file. For a logical file, the VALUES keyword can also be specified at the select- or omit-field level, or both.

☐ Hint: The VALUES keyword also applies to physical files and logical files when specified at the field level for validity checking in display files.

VALUES Function and Form

The VALUES keyword is used in the select/omit level with either a select (S) or Omit (O) option specified in column 17. It works very similarly to the COMP operation. However, instead of one value being tested, or a range of values being tested, a list of values is tested. The select/omit rules described under COMP also apply to VALUES.

The format of the keyword is:

VALUES(value-1 [value-2...[value-100]])

VALUES Example

The following example shows a complete set of complete DDS for a logical file. However, the DDS from statements 20 to 40 are coded the same for a physical file. In this respect, for a physical or a logical file, these statements represent coding being done on behalf of a later to-be-built display file. If the PFILE keyword were removed from the record line (00010) in the sample code below, and lines 50 and 60 were also removed, this would be all be valid code for using the VALUES keyword with a physical file.

```
0010A R RECRD1     PFILE(PF1)
0020A   FIELDA 1 0 VALUES(1 6 9)
0030A   FIELDB 1   VALUES('A' 'B' 'C')
0040A K FIELDB
0050A S FIELDB     VALUES('A' 'B')
0060A S FIELDA     VALUES(1 6) 2
```

VALUES at the Field Level

In this example, you would code the VALUES (statements 00020 and 00030) as specified for FIELDA and FIELDB for later display file validity checking purposes. At the field level in a physical or logical file, the use of the VALUES is limited as a keyword for display files that later refer to FIELDA and FIELDB. In the display file that would later be built, when this VALUES keyword is in control of a field on a display, it requires that the work station user type only 1, 6, or 9 in FIELDA or an A, B, or C in FIELDB. FIELDA is an example of coding a numeric field and FIELDB is an example of coding a character field. All of the information in this paragraph pertains to both physical and logical files.

VALUES at the Select/Omit Level

For logical files, You would also code the VALUES keyword at statements 00050 and 00060, if you were using those values for selecting or omitting records via a logical file. It is not at first obvious that statements 00020 and 00060 above are not mutually exclusive. Additionally. Statements 00030 and 00050 are not mutually exclusive. They mean different things.

As you can see in this example, on statements 00050 and 00060, VALUES is specified as a select/omit keyword for FIELDA. Moreover, on statements 00030 and 00050, VALUES is specified as a select/omit keyword for FIELDB. As a point of note, the two select omit statements at 00050 and 00060 form an OR condition, not AND. Therefore, records from the physical file PF1 are retrieved through this logical file record format only if the value of FIELDA is 1, 6 or 9 or the value of FIELDB is A, B, or C. The Values keyword on statements 00020 and 0030 are for later use.

Chapter 13   Logical File Coding Examples - Non Join Format Operations

LF DDS Coding Example - Projection

Now that we have reviewed the level keywords for logical file DDS, let's move on to a bit of logical file coding that uses a number of these keywords. At the same time, we'll give more detailed explanations of some keywords we have already used - in the context of the examples.

☐ Note: In order to correctly explain Dynamic Select (DYNSLT), just about all other aspects of non-join and join files needs to be reasonably understood. Therefore, we dedicated a whole Chapter 15 for this purpose. To present the forthcoming examples in th best light, you will find the DYNSLT keyword used where it makes sense. It is a chicken / egg situation. As appropriate in these examples, we describe the functions of the DYNSLT in context without describing DYNSLT per se.

Figure F-21 DDS Logical File - Some Fields

```
A* Logical FILE (PRINQRY)
A                                              DYNSLT
A    R  PRINQRYR
PFILE(HELLO/EARNMAST)
            EMPNAM
            EMPINL
            RATE
            EMPNO
            STATUS

      K   EMPNAM
      S   STATUS                          COMP(EQ  'D')
```

PFILE Keyword in Example

The PFILE parameter in Figure F-21 says that the
EARNMAST file in HELLO is the physical file upon which
this logical file named PRINQRY is based. The PFILE
keyword is used to code the physical file(s) and the library
(optional), upon which the logical file being defined is to be
built.

Relational Projection

The rule for fields in logical files is that either (1) you specify no
fields at all and then you get all fields in your logical view, or
(2) you specify each of the fields that you want in your view
and do not specify those fields that you do not want in your
view. It's all or nothing but specified.

Subset Fields and / or Rearrange

This is how DDS provides the relational projection operation
which is the moral equivalent of the Create View command in
SQL. In addition to being able to project a subset of the fields,
you might also choose to rearrange the fields. You must specify
all of the fields you want in the view in the sequence that you
want your record to be projected.

Let's suppose you do not want to subset fields. You merely want to change the order of one or two fields in the record layout using the logical view, you must specify all of the other fields you want to be in the view. For example, let's say you wanted to switch the record position of the EMPNAM and EMPNO fields. In order to also have all of the other fields in the view, you would have to specify each of the other fields in the field sequence in the record format as you desired. The moral is that when you define or change the position of just one field, you have to specify them al l— to get them all in the view.

Relational Order

Relational order is achieved in this set of DDS via the K in position 17 next to the EMPNAM field. This Key level field name defines the key for the file. If more than one key is desired for the file (composite key), then more key field entries can be used. The most important keys must be specified first in order to achieve the desired record sequence. As you can see this view is sequenced by EMPNAM (Employee name). HLL programs can randomly or sequentially access this logical using the key regardless of whether the physical file was built with a key.

☐ Hint You cannot use a field which you are not projecting (in the logical file record format) as a key field. If you project no fields and you therefore get all fields, you can select any field in the physical file as the key. In this case, all fields from the physical are also fields in the logical view. If, however, you use subset of the physical file fields as the fields for the logical view, you cannot use a field which is not in the logical file as the key for that file.

Relational Selection

The last statement in Figure F-21 is the select / omit level for the DDS. This is how relational selection is provided in DDS. In the Select/Omit level, you use the DDS select / omit keywords (COMP, RANGE, VALUES) along with the S and O level codes to specify your record selection criteria. In the example in Figure F-21, as you can see, only the records in which the status codes are equal to the letter "D" are visible.

The keyword, DYNSLT tells the database that the selection criteria for this file should not be maintained immediately. Instead, the status "D" records are selected at run time. In this way, the database does not have to work keeping this access path up to date when there are no programs using the logical file. Thus, records are selected dynamically in Employee name sequence, with only the five projected fields delivered in this view.

Record Format Names

In the Logical file DDS in Figure F-21, the comment suggests that the logical file created from this DDS will be named PRINQRY. The PFILE keyword says it will be built over the Physical File EARNMAST. The logical file format name we selected is PRINQRYR. This is merely the file name with an "R" at the end. It could have been given any name as long as fields are defined for the format. If no fields were specified, which means that all fields from physical are to be used, the format name used for the logical file, would have to be the same name as the format name in the physical file. There is one more possibility regarding the format name. You can also use the name of a format in another file. In this case, however, you would need to specify the DDS FORMAT command which is covered in Chapter 9 under the heading FORMAT, as well as below.

LF DDS Coding Example - Order, No Projection

Now, let's examine and in some cases, reexamine the logical file record format level keywords, such as PFILE, TEXT, and FORMAT as they exist in some live logical files – at least in the DDS.

Figure F-22 represents DDS with these keywords.

Figure F-22 DDS Logical File - all fields

```
A* Logical FILE  (PRMASTL1)
A*
A     R   EARNMSTR
PFILE(PREARNMAST)
      K   EMPNO
```

Logical File Name

This DDS code in Figure F-22 is more like the way most developers code their logical files. A logical file, frightening as it may be initially to understand, is a piece of cake to code in its most simplistic form. Here it is before you in Figure F-22. If it were not for the comments noting the based on physical file, there would be just two DDS statements.

☐ Hint: By the way, The association of the physical file name with the DDS occurs with the CRTLF command. Nothing in DDS links the file to the DDS. Therefore, it is a good convention (shop standard) to present the file name in a comment within the DDS for that file.

Record Format Name

Unless a different projected relational view is required, you get a full logical file with the coding in Figure F-22. By specifying no fields (no projection) in your logical file, you get all the fields in your new view. Notice that the format name which is used is EARNMSTR. It is the format in the physical file (PFILE) EARNMAST.

By specifying this format name on the record level line(R in 17) , you are telling the DDS compiler to take a trip to the physical file format EARNMSTR within the file object EARNMAST (not the physical file's DDS),at compile time, to rustle up all the fields for this new logical view. It's a lot easier to write than that last sentence. It saves you a lot of unnecessary coding and that is its main purpose.

The link to all of the fields in the format by specifying the format name of the physical file in the DDS "R" (record format) specification line. When you specify the right format name for the physical file, you get all of its fields. It's that simple. The DDS compiler copies them from the physical file object into the format of the logical file. Therefore, if you want all the fields, there is no need to specify any fields when the logical file will include all of the fields.

Key Field

If you look again at Figure F-22, you will notice that the last line is a Key-Field level "K" entry. As you would expect, this is where the key is provided — or keys are provided — depending on the file. In this case, the key is EMPNO. The system will build an access path for this key if it finds none suitable to share. Otherwise, it will latch onto and share an existing access path if one exists from another logical file or even the EARNMAST physical file's keyed access path. Of course, if the physical file were already in key sequence by

EMPNO, there would be little need for this Key-Level or this logical file for that matter.

Remove Key Field

If we were to remove the key field specification for this file, would the DDS continue to represent a viable logical file. Yes, it would! Of course, to create a logical file, we would have to compile the DDS. This DDS will most certainly compile, even though there is just one live statement. It happens that the statement has a PFILE so it knows the based-on physical. It also has a record format level "R" named EARNMSTR which can be found in the physical file. The resulting logical file would not have a keyed access path but it would process the data (all fields) from the EARNMAST physical file in arrival sequence. There may not be much use for this type of one statement logical file, but it sure helps give an appreciation for how logical files work, what is essential, and what is not.

Fields Made Part of LF Format

It is good to remember that the logical file does not borrow the record format of the physical file at execution time. Nor does it continually point to the record format of the physical file No Sir–ee Bob! It has its own record format as part of the logical file object. Where does it get it? At compile time, it goes to the physical file object and gets all of the information it needs from the referenced format and it brings it into the logical file.

LF DDS Coding Example- Order With Projection

Figure F-23 shows another simple example of projection over the EARNMAST file. This time the image projected is of just two fields: employee name and employee initial. The file is ordered by employee name (EMPNAM) as per the key level statement with the EMPNAM field repeated.

Figure F-23 Simple Logical File With Projection and Order

```
A* Logical FILE (PROJPRL)
A*
A      R   PROJECTN          PFILE(HELLO/EARNMAST)
           EMPNAM
           EMPINL
       K   EMPNAM
```

Notice that only EMPNAM and EMPINL are the only two fields included in the projection (view) in Figure F-23. A program using this view in its file description would receive only these two fields for input and/or output use. The HLL (RPG, COBOL) compiler does not see the other fields in the underlying physical file.

LF DDS Coding Example - Union & Order with Projection

Now, let's try another relational operation, UNION. In the next two examples, you have an old master file and a new master file and the objective is to marry (logically merge or union) the two files using fields that are common to them both.

Relational Union versus Relational Join

Unlike a join which we will be studying shortly, the result of a UNION is a view of similar data in multiple files as if they were all lumped together, and then sorted by the union key level field. In other words, if there were a three file union and each of the three physical files had thirty-three records, the union view would have ninety nine records – all sorted together like one big homogenous file view.

We can contrast Union with Join even before we study Join. If, for example, you joined the same three files. Assume for this instance that you know that the data is perfect and that the resulting Join would produce a logical file that which was really a natural, inner, and matching join (three names for the same thing). In other words, there would be a record in each of the secondary's for each primary record.

If this were all true, then after the join, the resulting view would not show 99 records as in the Union example. Instead it would show just thirty-three records. As a friend of mine would say "Combinatorically speaking, the Join combines the records into one record." Therefore, each record would show a piece (one or several fields) from each of the physical files which were joined.

Figure F-24 DDS LF - UNION - Some Fields

```
A* Logical FILE (PRUNSOME)
A*
A      R   PRUNSOMR       PFILE(EARNMAST OLDEARN)
           EMPNAM
           EMPINL
           RATE
           EMPNO
           STATUS
       K   EMPNO

From Two, One
```

Union takes two almost identically structured files and combines them. A good example is that shown in Figure F-24 in which there are New Masters and Old Masters. The new combined view of the data (PRUNSOMR) includes only the named (projected) fields from all records in both the old Payroll Earnings Master (OLDEARN)and the new Payroll Earnings Master (EARNMAST). Overall, up to 32 files can be unioned.

Though there are two files defined in the PFILE, without library qualifiers, this is not a join since there is no Join Record Format (J in column 17). Each record contains data from just one physical file, not both as in a join. A key field (EMPNO in this case) must be specified in a UNION.

LF DDS Coding Example- Union, Order No Projection

In Figure F-25, we show a UNION with all fields.

Figure F-25 DDS LF - UNION - all fields

```
A* LOGICAL FILE  (PRUNALL)
A*
A          R EARNMSTR PFILE(EARNMAST OLDEARN)
           K EMPNO
```

Figure F-25 includes all fields from all records in both the old Payroll Master and the New Payroll master. Notice the format name is EARNMAST. This says that the union will use the format (all the fields) of the new master file. There cannot be any extra fields in EARNMAST compared to OLDEARN. All fields in EARNMAST must also exist in OLDEARN. If there are any such differences in these two files, the logical file will not compile and it will produce severe error messages and it will not be created.

LF DDS Coding Example- Reformat and Order with no Projection

Now, let's try a new wrinkle on Union. Let's use a Format keyword to reformat the UNIONed data. In the next example, we assume that we have added a new field to the new earnings file and we want a unioned view of the fields in the OLDEARN file. This does not contain the new field. This may be something you would do to accommodate consolidations, etc., so that you can get the known information from two similar groups of records. Take a look at the DDS in Figure F-26, and ask yourself if it has a new format? If so, what format is that?

In the example in Figure F-26, you see another UNION but this time assume that the files have different formats. Since we still want the records UNIONED, you are going to have to select a format which has fields that exist in both files to govern the new UNIONed view.

Figure F-26 DDS LF - UNION - Format

```
A*  LOGICAL FILE  (UNALLFMT)
A*
A           R OLDEARNR     PFILE(EARNMAST OLDEARN)
                           FORMAT(OLDEARN)
            K EMPNO
```

This new logical view of data called UNALLFMT, uses the format of the old earnings file. Both the old and the new earnings file have all of the fields of the new EARNMAST file. Assume we have just added the PAYCOD field to the EARNMAST file. We cannot use the EARNMSTR format for the union since there is no PAYCOD field in the OLDEARN file.

This new format shares the OLDEARNR format from the old Payroll Master File. Fields from the new master which are not in the old format are not included in the new Unioned view called UNALLFMT.

LF DDS Coding Example- Simple, Non-Join Multiple Format Logical File

Now, we have an even newer wrinkle. As part of our continuing saga of presenting non-join solutions for your approval, we leave the unions behind and move on to a non-join, non-union example set. Again this example uses two physical database files. They will not be joined and they will not be unioned.

Multiple Formats - One Set of DDS

Instead, one logical file will be built over the two physicals. The end result is that both formats, one from each physical file, will be present in the new view. Rather than bore you by showing all the physical file detail, we can assume that, in addition to the EARNMAST file, our payroll system also has a timecard file called TIMECARD. The full description of the TIMECARD file is given in Chapter 8. The file has a number of important fields such as employee number and number of hours worked. It also has one record format, the name of which is TIMECDR.

In a payroll application, it does not make sense to join a timecard record to a master record. After all, a time card is a transaction record that has a life of about one payroll period. Next pay period there will be a new record. However, most payrolls are processed by reading the time card and then reading the master record. Wouldn't it be nice if you could fashion a logical file over both the employee master file and the time card file so that the records would arrive in the typical way payrolls are processed?

Link by a Common Field

Well, you can! By using a common field which exists in both files, you can define each format with a key field, such as employee number. It doesn't matter if the key in one format is named EMPNO and in the next it is EMP#. What matters is that a common field exists and that the attributes of the fields are the same.

By defining the time card file first in DDS, as in Figure F-27, you can create a logical view in which the time card record is presented first followed by the master record. By using the same employee number key on both files, the two files would behave as if they had been merged.

Proper Order, Intermixed Records

Therefore, a program could rightly expect that after the time card record for say, employee 300 was processed the next record read in the program would be the employee record for . . . you guessed it . . . employee 300. Unless the master were missing, which creates a processing issue in all cases, the master record for an employee would always be processed immediately after the time card record for the same employee. It's simple. It's just the way it works.

Since the format of the time card record is different from the format of the master record, the logical file built over these is known as a multiple-format logical file. The resulting view therefore has two formats, not one format as in the Union examples above and in the Join examples to come.

HLL Program Processing

The HLL program to process this logical file, would need just one file defined - the multiple format logical file (MULTPRTC in this example). The program would read from the one logical file and would process both records separately — the time card record followed by the payroll master record.

The AS/400 database is the only relational database which provides a multi-format view of data. Another name for this is a hierarchical view, and it is the most favorite view presented by hierarchical databases, which were the predecessors of relational DBS.

Check Out the DDS

When you examine the DDS in Figure F-27, you will notice
that there are multiple record format level "R" statements
defined. Since you want multiple formats in the logical file
(time card and master) you would need to be able to define the
separate formats (TIMECDR and EARNMSTR) for both
physical files within in the same set of DDS. Moreover, the
format names are the same and must be the same names as the
formats in the underlying physical files.

Ladies and Gentlemen, the view we have been waiting for is
now available in Figure F-27.

Figure F-27 Multiple-Format LF - Non-Union, Non-Join

```
A* Logical FILE (MULTPRTC)
A*

A      R   TIMECDR                        PFILE(TIMECD)
       K   EMPNO
A      R   EARNMSTR                       PFILE(EARNMAST)
       K   EMPNO
```

Compatibility View

This hierarchical view of the Payroll Master and the timecard
files is a database extension for compatibility with non database
systems (multiple record types in the same file). Up to 32 files
can be logically "merged" in this fashion. That means you can
have up to 32 formats — one record format per physical file
defined within one set of DDS and linked by a common key
field.

Each record, when processed, provides data from just one
physical file at a time. A key field must be specified for the
logical "merge" to take place.

LF DDS Coding Example- Multiple Format Logical File - Complex

To round out our coverage of multiple-format logical files, let's up the ante a bit. To get going, let's take a look at a logical view over three physical files with some of the key fields missing. See Figure F-28 to observe the coding for this nifty trick.

In the example, there are clearly three files specified. In the DDS coding, you can see that each grouping (between each record format – R in position 17) represents the coding for one physical file. Even without knowing all of the specifics, such as all of the field names in the physical file, you can code this logical file, or at least you can be in a position to understand its coding. First, of course, you need to learn how the multiple format logical file object is constructed.

There is a piece of information about this example, and its new files (ADDRMAST and DEDMAST) that you would need to know to make all this make sense. We will reveal this information very shortly.

Physical File Definitions

For now, for your convenience, we have provided the physical file layouts for these two files in Figure F-29. You will see the DDS for both physical files in a consolidated DDS form. Additionally, if you want a better definition of these files, you can see their full record layout under the heading DDS Examples right at the end of
Chapter 8.

We have already seen a number of examples using the EARNMAST file and we have examined a detailed record layout and we have coded the DDS for the physical file as well as a number of based-upon logical files. However, you are not yet as familiar with the ADDRMAST and the DEDMAST files. Therefore, it may help for you, before you may choose to re-take a theory diversion, to examine the coding for the logical file and these two physical files in Figures F-28 and F-29.

At the end of Chapter 6, you will find a section called Formal Diversion - Database Theory. You may want to divert back there before you continue. When you do that, come aback and we'll say: "Now, let's go take that diversion!"

If you are already well familiar with formal entity relationship theory and data modeling, feel free to skip the section in Chapter 6, and proceed to the heading: The PRMULT File under the Return from Database Theory heading below.

Return from Database Theory

Go have a nice Coffee or a Gatorade or even a beer or some nice red wine to reward yourself for that head hurting theory activity from which you may have just returned. We are going to continue right where we left off with the complex multiple format logical file.

The PRMULT File

So what does all this theory have to do with the multiple format logical file we have displayed in Figure F-28. Now that you have seen the record layouts and we have discussed some database theory, hopefully this Figure will be much easier to understand.

The EARNMAST Component

Notice first that the area of DDS in which the EARNMAST file is described has but one primary key, the EMPNO field. The records are unique in that file based on EMPNO. That is not the case for the other two files.

The ADDRMAST Component

The ADDRMAST file, for example has a field in it called Line#. A person's address in the ADDRMAST file may take anywhere form three to 100 records to store all the lines of address. You might choose to put all of your address lines in one file, but, technically, there is a one to many relationship between an employee and a line of address. Thus, this design is relationally correct. With this design, of course, you can see why the Address Entity is not within the EARNMAST file.

Rather than have a repeating group inside the EARNMAST file, the designer chose to have each line of the address be in its own record. Because the line number field is numeric and it is two digits wide, there can be 100 lines of address (00 to 99) for each employee. If you think know you'd never need that many, then that is good design.

The EMPNO field and the LINE# field form what is called a composite key. Uniqueness cannot be achieved in this file without mashing both of these fields together. Since a major relational database precept (which can be violated with impunity on AS/400 and IBM i with DDS) is that you must have a primary (unique) ID for each record, the composite key of EMPNO and LINE# does the trick for the ADDRMAST file. These two keys together make the "key" unique.

The DEDMAST Component

Now, let's take the DEDMAST file. This guy also has a composite key. The first part is EMPNO and the second part is the deduction type. That is how each deduction type, for which an employee is signed up, is linked and is therefore unique to the particular employee. For example, consider EMPNO/DEDTYP = 000300UW. This would be the United Way deduction for employee number 300.

There are a number of different type deductions for Payroll such as United Way, Hospitalization, Bonds, etc. Thus each deduction has its own ID such as UW, HOSP, BOND, etc and the ID is stored in a 5-position alpha field. Together with EMPNO, a 6, 0 field, this makes each deduction record for each employee unique, thereby fulfilling the primary key rule.

Putting the Whole System Together

Now, let's say you are employee 321. Let's also say you have six lines of address. Thus each of these address lines, as the record layout shows, has EMPNO as well as LINE# in the record. Let's also say that you have two of the three deductions - codes UW & HOSP. These records would need EMPNO and DEDTYP in them.

File and Data Sequencing

Let's say one more thing before we shut up. In the process of designing the system, the analyst defined just one program. It needs all of the address records to be processed immediately after the EARNMAST record. The last of these ADDRMAST line records is to be followed by the DEDMAST records for each employee, one employee at a time. Thus the sequence of records for employee 321 is as follows:

Primary Key		Physical File
000321	from	EARNMAST
00032101	from	ADDRMAST
00032102	from	ADDRMAST
00032103	from	ADDRMAST
00032104	from	ADDRMAST
00032105	from	ADDRMAST
00032106	from	ADDRMAST
000321HOSP	from	DEDMAST
000321UW	from	DEDMAST

From One File, Many Formats

The analyst also wants the programmer to use just one file in the program to access the data from these three files. The only way the data from multiple files could be processed through one file definition in a program is if the file is a multiple format logical file - period. Your job is to take the analysts system design and do the database magic. You get to specifically design and code the logical file that can make that set of requirements actually happen.

Les Voila! You already did it and your coding for it is in Figure F-28. Thanks for a great job!

Figure F-28 DDS Multi-Format LF- More Than 2 Physicals

```
A* Logical FILE (PRMULT)
A                                    UNIQUE    (LIFO,
FIFO)
A*
A       R    EARNMSTR                PFILE(EARNMAST)
        K    EMPNO
        K    *NONE
        K    *NONE

        R    ADDRMSTR                PFILE(ADDRMAST)
        K    EMPNO
        K    LINE#
        K    *NONE

        R    DEDMASTR                PFILE(DEDMAST)
        K    EMPNO
        K    *NONE
        K    DEDTYP
```

Figure F-29 Address & Deduction Masters– Physical File DDS

```
A* PAYROLL NAME AND ADDRESS MASTER
A             R ADDRMSTR                    TEXT('ADDRESS MASTER')
                EMPNO        6   0          COLHDG('EMPLOYEE NUMBER')
                LINE#        2S  0          COLHDG('ADDRESS LINE #')
                ADLINE       40             COLHDG('ADDRESS LINE DATA')
              K EMPNO
              K LINE#
              K ADLINE
```

```
A* PAYROLL DEDUCTION MASTER
A             R DEDMSTR                     TEXT('ADDRESS MASTER')
                EMPNO        6   0          COLHDG('EMPLOYEE NUMBER')
                DEDTYP       5              COLHDG('DEDUCTION TYPE')
                DEDDSC       40             COLHDG('DED DESCRIPTION')
                DEDAMT       6   2          COLHDG('DEDUCTION AMOUNT')
                DEDFRQ       2S  0          COLHDG('DED FREQUENCEY')
              K EMPNO
              K DEDTYP
```

Analyzing the DDS Code

In Figure F-28, the first step is to line up your formats. All three
format records are in tact in the figure, referencing the proper
format name in the underlying physical files. The PFILE
keywords are also accurate. Each reflects the correct physical
file. The order of the record formats is right also. How do we
know this? Well, the specs say that all of the address records
should sit in between the EARNMAST records and the
deduction records. They will in this circumstance.

Format Placement

The placement of the formats is critical to achieving this. When
there is a match on the most important key value, the primary
record (first record format described) is processed first, followed
by the first secondary file, followed by the next secondary file,
etc. Was it luck? Maybe! Don't matter though! It is correct.

*NONE Key Fields

Now, how about those darn key fields containing the
"*NONEs?" Well, the system cannot merge keys that do not
have the same attributes. The first thing to do is to try to figure

out how many keys are involved. Since there are three different key fields, it is pretty easy. There will be three slots. The first key, EMPNO, will exist in the first slot for all of the record formats. It is present in all three files and it has the same attributes in all files.

EARNMAST Specifications

If you take a look at the primary file - EARNMAST file – the first file specified – you quickly notice that there are no LINE# or DEDTYP fields present in the format. They exist only in the ADDRMAST and DEDMAST files, respectively. To accommodate this, DDS permits you to put in the "*NONEs." For EARNMAST it means *NONE in the second and third key positions.

ADDRMAST Specifications

The same goes for the address file which is the second file to be specified. You know there are three key slots. There are just two key slots needed to order and make the ADDRMAST file unique. One of them is EMPNO and the other is LINE#. LINE# therefore becomes the second key in the logical file. Since ADDRMAST has no third key, you just say "*NONE" in the third key position.

This coding says that when there is a match on employee number with EARNMAST, the database should provide a sorted view of the ADDRMAST records using LINE#. In this way, the logical view presents line 1 before it presents line 2, then it presents line 2 before it presents line 3, etc.

DEDMAST Specifications

The DDS coding processes the DEDMAST file in similar fashion. In this case, there is no LINE# field in the DEDMSTR format, yet the slot for LINE# is already taken. So, how do you accommodate this? You specify *NONE in the DEDMSTR format for the second key since there is no LINE# in the DEDMAST file.

Since there is just one key slot left, the DEDTYP field is specified in the DEDMAST file. Two key slots are already occupied. Since EMPNO and LINE# do not mean the same thing nor are their attributes the same, they cannot exist at the same key slot. We say *NONE in the second key position since the second level key for the file is already occupied by a 2-position numeric LINE# field. The DEDMAST file has no such field. Therefore, for DEDMAST, you use the third key level position to specify ordering by the DEDTYP field.

This says that whenever we have an EMPNO match among the three files or between the EARNMAST file and the DEDMAST file, the database should provide a sorted view of the deduction records using the DEDTYP field.

How About *NONE for DEDTYP

If you specify *NONE in the third key slot of the DEDMAST DDS, the DDS compiler would bomb since, in the third key-slot, each file would provide *NONE. You must have at least one real key in a key slot. Therefore, if you really would like to specify *NONE instead of DEDTYP and you are willing to let the deduction records arrive in random sequence within EMPNO, you can reduce the number of key slots to two. If you do not care about the order of the DEDMAST records, you would use only two key levels for the file.

Review

Let's take a quick review. For any multiple format logical file, you can always count on at least one thing. There will be one format for each physical file. Though this idea may be intuitive, there is something about multiple format logical files that at first looks formidable. Having this one rule in mind will certainly help you get started in coding the DDS for any multiple format logical file.

It follows that you will have as many record format level ("R" in column17) in your DDS as you have physical files. In fact, each physical file will have to be coded in your DDS by specifying the name of its format on the "R" level specification as well the PFILE statement which names the physical file for that particular record.

Though the presence of the *NONE entries above in Figure F-28 complicate the picture somewhat, the notion of multiple physical files can appear to be more simple than it first seems. Look again if you would at the coding for each referenced physical file - EARNMAST – Earnings Master, ADDRMAST – Name and Address Master, and DEDMAST – Deduction Master.

In Figure F-28, each physical file is coded as it would be if there were no other physical files. So, if you can envision coding each physical file from its "R" spec to its last key-field level statement on a separate piece of paper, or a separate panel, it can simplify your approach to creating the DDS for all of the files in a multiple format logical file. Do each one separately and then bring them together. When you have multiple key levels, just specify *NONE as a place holder when the file you are describing has no field for a certain key value.

Composite Key

In this section, the three key slots represented what is called a composite key. You need a composite key when there is more than one field in a file which is needed to provide unique (no duplicates) access to a physical file.

LF DDS Coding Example- Simple, Non-Join, Rename a
Format

Now, it is time to move on to a new function – the last new
function being introduced for this chapter. Let's rename a
format in a logical view. The coding for this is very similar to
the UNION with the OLDEARNR format from F-26. The new
code is shown in
Figure F-30

Figure F-30 DDS Logical File - Rename Format

```
A*  Logical FILE (RNMFORMAT)
A*
A        R RNMFORMATR                        PFILE(EARNMAST)
                                             FORMAT(EARNMSTR)
K    EMPNO
```

The technique in Figure F-30 is used when the logical file and
the physical over which it is built are defined in the same
program. Both files must have different format names when
used in the same program. Since many HLL operations, such
as READ and WRITE are performed against the Format name
rather than the file name, this tool provides a way to remove
the confusion for the HLL compiler.

Operations to one format (RNMFORMATR) would be for the
logical file (RNMFORMAT) and operations against the other
format (EARNMSTR) would be for the physical file. The
Format statement informs the DDS compiler to create a new
format for this logical file and to use the EARNMSTR format
as the basis. The new format name (RNMFORMATR) is
specified on the first record level line along with the PFILE for
EARNMAST.

Chapter 14   Logical File Coding Examples - Non Join Field Operations

LF DDS Coding Example - Rename Fields

Moving right along in our DDS expose, let's now learn how to rename fields in DDS. Check out the DDS in Figure F-31.

Figure F-31 Renaming Fields in Logical File

```
A* Logical FILE  (PRRENAMEF)
A*
A      R PRRENAMEFR                    PFILE(EARNMAST)
         NAME                          RENAME(EMPNAM)
         INL                           RENAME(EMPINL)
         EMPINL
           . . .
       K EMPNO
```

First, notice the convention for naming the file within DDS comments – PRRENAMEFR This represents the payroll logical file with renamed fields. This is a new record format because the view is not the same as the structure of the physical file. This is a projected view. The name for this new format is

PRRENAMEFR.

The coding in Figure F-31 renames the physical file field EMPNAM to NAME for use in this logical view. The field named EMPINL is also renamed to INL for this logical view. The next line shows the field EMPINL as the third field in the projected view. Though there may not be much practical use for this particular example, it does show that you can create views that provide multiple field names for the same space in the record. In this example, INL and EMPINL will point to the same storage location in a program.

Handy for Program Conversion

This technique can come in handy if you are converting some old programs from System/3 or System/34 or System/36 or System/36 environment to native database access. If your programs have several names for the same field, you can rename the field as many times as you would like. When you convert your program to use the external description from the database, the internal fields in various programs can use the same names as when the data was internally described as long as you rename the field and include all the renamed field in the format sued in your programs.

LF DDS Coding Example - Concatenation and Substrings

Now let's move to Figure F-32 where we do some fancy stuff like concatenate and substring some physical file fields for use in a logical view. When you do this, the user of the logical sees one big field instead of several small ones for concatenations, and sees smaller fields for substrings.

Figure F-32 DDS LFe-CONCAT & SUBSTRING fields

```
A* Logical FILE (PRCATSST)
*
A R   PRCATSSTR          PFILE(EARNMAST)
      NAME               CONCAT(EMPINL EMPNAM)
      RATE
      SEQDAT             CONCAT(YR MO DA)
      PRTDAT             CONCAT(MO DA YR)
      STREET       I     SST(ADDR1 4 21)
      . . .
  K   EMPNO
```

Again, you can see the convention for naming the file within DDS comments – PRCATSST. This represents a payroll logical file with concatenated and sub stringed fields. There is a new record format because the view is not the same as the structure of the physical file. This is a projected view. The name for this new format is PRCATSSTR, which uses the file name plus "R" convention.

Concatenation for Name

There are three concatenations defined for Figure F-32. From the top, the first CONCAT takes initial and name and brings them together into one field called NAME. There are no blanks between the fields, unless they are within the fields.

Concatenation for Sequence Date

The next field is the RATE, followed by SEQDAT. The SEQDAT field (date for sequencing) is formed from a concatenation of fields YR, MO, and DA (year, month day). This permits a year first date which can be used for sorting by date.

Concatenation for Print / Display Date

The PRTDAT field concatenates the same three date fields: MO, DA, and YR, but in a different sequence. These are combined to create a normal date format for printing.

Substring Street

The next field in the projected view is the street name. This field is formed by sub-stringing the ADDR1 field, hoping to capture the street name in position four. You may rightly suggest this is a bogus substring, and you are correct.

In the substring of the street field, the coder is assuming that the street number is three positions (probably not a good assumption) and that the real street starts at position four for a length of 21 characters. The result of the substring of field ADDR1 is stored in a new field which exists only in the logical called STREET.

This example may have more value if you create a few other views of this file in addition to this view, and each view showed the street name starting at a different position in the record, theoretically all the street names could be captured in perhaps as few as six different views. You could then write a simple program which created a new physical file which contained only the records from the six views which did not contain a blank or a number in position one of the record.

The number of records in the resulting physical file would approximate, if not be exactly the number of records in the based-on physical file. The street name would be a real field without the number. Such work can be helpful in file conversions as well as in applications for government jurisdictions in which street is an important element.

Concatenation and Substring Rules

As you would expect, there may be instances where everything that is concatenated or sub-stringed does not look as you would expect or you can't really do what you want with the data. There are a few simple rules to follow to get the most from these tools:

Some more boring rules / reminders are appropriate at this time. The rules for concatenated fields include the following:

1. You can concatenate any character field with no issue.

2. When concatenating any zero decimal position numeric field, the sign of the rightmost field is the sign which is used.

3. Numeric concatenations always convert to zoned decimal form, not packed decimal and the size limit is 31 digits maximum.

The following rules apply for substring fields:

1. If the field on the SST keyword is hexadecimal, the resulting field is hexadecimal; otherwise, the resulting field is always character. If the data type is not specified in DDS, a default of H or A is assigned.

2. The use of the resulting field must be either input-only (I) or neither (N).

3. The length of the resulting field is optional. You must specify either the field length or the length parameter on the keyword. If you specify both, they must be equal. If the field length is not specified, it is assigned the length parameter on the keyword.

4. You cannot specify this keyword on the same field with the CONCAT, RENAME, or TRNTBL keywords.

5. The field specified on this keyword cannot be defined with the CONCAT, TRNTBL, or SST keywords

LF DDS Coding Example - Changing Field Lengths

While we are playing with the look and feel of fields in a logical file projection, let's get even simpler than concatenation and substring. Wouldn't it be nice if you could change the projected length of some fields so that their view is different from the underlying reality.

Of course, you must remember when using this type of projection that the underlying physical still stores all the data. No matter how big or small you make a logical field, if there is no room for data from the real field to be projected, you will get an error in your HLL program when it tries to use a misshaped projection.

Figure F-33 DDS LF - Change Field Lengths

```
A*  Logical FILE  (CHGLEN)
A*
A   R   CHGLENR                    PFILE(EARNMAST)
        EMPNAM        21
        EMPINL
         RATE         +2   3
        SALARY        +2  +1
        EMPNO
        STATUS
    K   EMPNO
```

In the example code, we continue the convention for naming the file within DDS comments – CHGLEN. This represents a payroll logical file with field lengths changed in the view. There is a new record format because the view is not the same as the structure of the physical file. This is a projected view. The name for this new format is CHGLENR, which uses the file name plus "R" convention.

You can also see that we changed the length of three different fields as projected by this view. We reduced EMPNAM to 21 positions from 25. We increased RATE two positions to eight. And we increased its # of decimals from two to three. We also increased SALARY in size by two positions. One of the positions is to be used for additional decimals. Though this is neat and can be very helpful, I repeat that you must be careful when writing through the logical that you do not send data which the physical file cannot handle.

As you can see, the length and decimal positions for the logical view can be specified in two different ways - by direct specification or by addition and/or subtraction. The EMPNAM field, for example is hard coded with a 21, even though the physical data length is 25. This may make the field more usable for queries when the user does not want to shorten fields within the Query – so he or she can fit more data on one line.

The RATE field is coded with a +2 for the length and a three for the number of decimals. As you may recall from the EARNMAST DDS, the RATE is defined as six (length), two (decimals). The plus two would make it eight (length), two (decimals). However, the logical overrides the number of decimals to three making the new projected view as eight (length), three (decimals).

The SALARY field is coded with a +2 for the length and a +1 for the number of decimals. As you may recall from the EARNMAST DDS, there was no SALARY field. We made it up for this example. Let's assume it would be seven (length), two (decimals). The plus two would make it nine (length), two (decimals). However, the logical overrides the number of decimals by +1 making the new projected view as nine (length), three (decimals).

Chapter 15   Logical File Coding Examples - Key Level and Select/Omit Level Keywords

Key-Level Keywords

Moving down the logical level hierarchy from fields, our next stop is key-field level keywords. As noted previously, the key field level keywords for logical files are: ABSVAL, DESCEND, DIGIT, NOALTSEQ, SIGNED, and UNSIGNED. The use of these keywords for a logical file is exactly the same as for a physical file definition.

LF DDS Coding Example - Using Composite Keys

In Figure F-34, we introduce the notion of coding more than one key field for a simple logical file join..

Figure F-34 Multiple Key Fields

```
A* Logical FILE (TWOKEY)
A*
A       R TWOKEYR              PFILE(EARNMAST)
          EMPNAM
          EMPINL
          RATE
          EMPNO
        K RATE
        K EMPNAM
```

You can see the convention for naming the file within DDS comments – TWOKEY. This example DDS represents a payroll logical file with a composite key. There is a new record format because the view is not the same as the structure of the physical file. This is a projected view. The name for this new format is TWOKEYR, which uses the logical file name plus "R" convention.

Just as there were rules for concatenation, and there are rules for just about everything else, even though rules are boring, we now present to you some of the rules for key fields.

1. One or more fields can comprise a key or composite key.

2. Key fields can be noncontiguous.

3. Back when the AS/400 was invented, the key length maximum was 256 BYTES. Now, the number of fields that make up a key is restricted to 120 and the total key length cannot exceed 2000 bytes (1995 bytes If you are using FCFO).

4. Key field must be in, or it's based on field (RENAME, et.) must be in the both physical and the logical file.

5. You cannot sequence on a field that is not projected for the logical view.

Now that we have become smart about keys, there really is little more we can say about keys. So, let's move on to some examples in the most exciting part of non-join logical file access - the select and omit level

LF DDS Coding Example - Simple Select Records

There are three select/omit level keywords which can be used in a logical file to reduce the number of records returned (selected) in a query. These are: COMP, a.k.a. CMP, RANGE, and VALUES. Let's start our examination of selection with the DDS in Figure F-35.

Figure F-35 DDS Logical File - Select records

```
A* Logical FILE  (SELKEY)
A*
A      R SELKEYR
PFILE(EARNMAST)
         EMPNO
         EMPNAM
         EMPINL
         RATE
         PAYCOD
      K EMPNO
      S PAYCOD                        COMP(EQ 'S')
```

You can see the convention for naming the file within DDS comments – SELKEY. This example DDS represents a payroll logical file with one select / omit statement, ordered by EMPNO. key. There is a new record format because the view is not exactly the same as the structure of the physical file. This is a projected view. The name for this new format is SELKEYR, which uses the logical file name plus "R" convention.

There is only one selection criterion in this example. As you can see it is the last statement in DDS. You can read this DDS statement as follows: "Select records where the pay code is "S."" Because there is no ALL keyword on an "S" or "O" (Column 17) statement, the default is to omit all of other records in which PAYCOD is not equal to "S.".

LF DDS Coding Example - Select Records with VALUES OR RANGE

Figure F-36 Select OR Relationship

```
A* Logical FILE (SEL2KEY)
A*
A        R SEL2KEYR       PFILE(EARNMAST)
           EMPNAM
           EMPINL
           RATE
           EMPNO
           PAYCOD
         K EMPNAM
         S EMPNO          VALUES(1 10 100 500)
         S EMPNO          RANGE(750 850)
```

You can see in Figure F-36 the convention for naming the file within DDS comments – SEL2KEY. This example DDS represents a payroll logical file with two ORed select / omit statements, ordered by the EMPNAM key. There is a new record format because the view is not exactly the same as the structure of the physical file. This is a projected view. The name for this new format is SEL2KEYR, which uses the logical file name plus "R" convention.

There are two selection criteria coded in the sample DDS. You read this set of DDS as follows: "Select records where the employee number is a 1, 10, 100, or 500. If the employee record does not get selected using this criteria, then select all of the employee records in which the EMPNO field is between 750 and 850."

This is an "OR" relationship. When two lines are to be "ORed" together, you repeat the "S" in the second and subsequent "ORed" select/omit line. An "AND" relationship would be coded as a blank (Range) on the second and subsequent select/omit records.

In this example, you are telling the database to include the record in the view if it is one of the listed values or if it is in the 750 to 850 range. Otherwise, since the ALL keyword is not coded and the last select/omit spec is a select, all other records are omitted and thus, will not appear in the view.

LF DDS Coding Example - Select / Omit Records with ALL

Figure F-37 shows several other select/omit relationships.

Figure F-37A DDS Logical File – S & O Records

```
A* Logical FILE (SELOKEY)
A*
A        R SELOKEYR              PFILE (EARNMAST)
           EMPNAM
           EMPINL
           EMPNO
           PAYCOD
           RATE
         K EMPNO
         S EMPNO                 COMP (EQ 550)
         O EMPNO                 RANGE (500 599)
         S                       ALL
```

You can see in Figure F-37A the convention for naming the file within DDS comments – SELOKEY. This example DDS represents a payroll logical file. There is a new record format which means that the view is not exactly the same as the structure of the physical file. Thus this is a projected view. The name for this new format is SELOKEYR, which uses the logical file name plus "R" convention.

This example has a Select statement and an Omit statement that are ORed together. If the first condition is not true and the record is not selected, then the second condition is tested. If the second test (RANGE test) is true, then the DDS says to omit the record. If neither the first nor the second test is true, then the S... ALL statement says to select all the remaining records when they are not specifically selected or omitted.

The relationship says to include records in the view for employee # 550 in all circumstances, but to omit all other employees in the 500 to 599 employee number range, and select all the rest.

LF DDS Coding Example - Select / Omit Records with And

Figure F-37B DDS Logical File – S & O Records

```
A* Logical FILE (SELAND)
A*
A       R SELANDR                  PFILE (EARNMAST)
          EMPNAM
          EMPINL
          EMPNO
          PAYCOD
          RATE
        K EMPNO
        S   RATE                   CMP (GT  4.45)
            RATE                   CMP (LT 12.35)
            TYPE                   CMP (EQ  'UNION')
```

You can see the convention for naming the file within DDS comments – SELAND – in Figure F-37B . This example DDS represents a payroll logical file. There is a new record format which pertains to both example DDS sets. The view is not exactly the same as the structure of the physical file. Thus this is a projected view. The name for this new format for both the top and bottom example is SELANDR, which uses the logical file name plus "R" convention.

This example says to include records in the view with a RATE that is greater than 4.45 and less than 12.35, and the type of employee is union. Reject all others from the view. Another way of saying this is that all union employees whose hourly rate is between 4.45 and 12.35 will be included in this view.

Creating a Logical File

Now, that we have covered all of the various levels (from record format to select/omit) that are involved in a non-join physical file, let's review the Create Logical File command one more time so we know how to get logical file objects created. The same CRTPF command also works when compiling JOIN logical file DDS.

The process to create a logical file is very similar to creating a physical file. It requires the following steps:

1. Invoke PDM to get your productivity list manager going,

2. Invoke option 2 of PDM which is SEU (STRSEU)

3. Name the member, in order to type your DDS specifications into a source file. Make sure you code the file as LF and not PF.

4. Use option 14 of PDM to compile the source and create the logical database file in a library of your choice. If you were to press the command prompter "F4" after typing in option 14 of PDM, the system would very nicely prompt you for all of the options on the CRTLF command. It would have the ones it could figure out from PDM already filled in for you. A sample of create physical file command you would see is given below:

```
CRTLF  FILE(HELLO/SELAND)
SRCFILE(HELLO/QDDSSRC) +
SRCMBR(*FILE) MBR(*FILE) DATAMBRS(*ALL)
MAXMBRS(1) +
TEXT(*SRCMBRTXT)
```

Chapter 16   Logical File Coding Examples - Join Keywords

Join Level Keywords

Application requirements are the determining factor as to which levels and which keywords should be used in a given project. The DDS keywords associated with the Join operation bring their own baggage to the mix. First of all, there is a Join Level in DDS at about the same hierarchical level as the record format. It is called the Join Record Format Level. Unfortunately, only two of the six Join keywords work at this level.

Therefore, we have provided a little chart right below which shows all six Join type keywords and it identifies the particular level in which the keyword can be specified.

Join Keyword Levels

Join Keyword	DDS Level
JFILE	Record Format
JOIN	Join Record Level
JDFTVAL	File Level
JDUPSEQ	Field Level
JFLD	Join Record Level
JREF	Field Level

Join File Level Keywords

JDFTVAL   Tells the join to provide default values for unmatched primaries. This is used to signal a left outer join type in which the database provides a record in the resulting view for every record in the primary file (first physical file defined). Default values of zeroes blanks or the database default are filled into the missing fields in the join format

Record Level Keywords

JFILE Names the Physical Files in the Join. Provide the names of the physical files (library name / file name) of the files that are to be included in the join. There can be up to 32 files in a Join.

Join Record Level Keywords

JOIN Specifies the sequence of the Joins. Use this join record level keyword to specify the sequence of the joins. These can be specified using file names or numbers which represent the sequence of the file in the JFILE statement

JFLD Specifies the link fields for the join. Use this join record level keyword to specify the linking fields in each of the files which are being joined.

Field Level Keywords

JDUPSEQ   Sort on this field when there are duplicates. Use this field level keyword to designate a field which should be used to control the order of the records when there is a duplicate.

JREF Tells the Join to use the field from this file. When two or more files in a join have the same field and it is a field which you are projecting, the JREF permits you to specify the specific based-on physical file from which the contents of that field are to be extracted when the database builds the Join format.

Detailed Look at the Join Keywords

JDFTVAL

You would use this Join logical file-level keyword (Join Default Values) so the system provides default values for fields when a join with a secondary file does not produce any records. In other words, use default values when there is an unmatched secondary

The format of JDFTVAL is quite easy since the keyword has no parameters. When you code your first joins, like us, you may think that the JDFTVAL keyword gets specified at the record level or join record level. This is not so. It gets specified at the file level.

The supplied default values for the database are blanks for character and hexadecimal fields and zeros for numeric fields. Of course, you can change the defaults for any of the fields specifying the DFT keyword for the fields when you define them in the physical file.

The beauty of the JDFTVAL keyword is that it gives DDS a left outer join facility. It has nothing to do with the notion of "left-out," however. Secondaries are not left out when you use the JDFTVAL. They are included. When you do not use the keyword JDFTVAL, any primary record which does not have a secondary record is left-out of the join. No default values are needed because neither the primary nor secondary records are included in the join record. The record does not make it into the view.

In a nutshell, if you specify JDFTVAL, your program retrieves all records from a primary file. All records are included in the view. W for which a secondary file does not have a corresponding record. Even records without a matching record in the join files are selected in the view. For these, the Join provides default values since there is no secondary record from which to get the data. If you do not specify JDFTVAL, a record in the primary file for which there is no corresponding record in a secondary file is skipped.

If you are joining two or more files, and you specify the JDFTVAL keyword for fields used as join fields, default values of fields missing in secondary files are used in the same way that a field value is used.

The AS/400 Database, DB2/400 does not support a full outer join nor does it support a right outer-join. Left outer join is left to right. Right outer join is built right file to left file. Full is both ways (left to right and right to left).

When you do a left outer join, for example, when all the left file records are joined to their matching right file record, unless there is a firm one to one relationship between the left and right files in the join, there more than likely are secondary (right file) records which are not selected to be in the final view. These would only be included if the AS/400 and IBM i database supported had a right-outer join or full outer join facility. One day as DB2/400 gets stronger, we may see right outer and full join facilities.

Example

The following example shows how to specify the JDFTVAL keyword.

```
00010A                JDFTVAL
00020A   R RCDR1      JFILE(PF1 PF2)
00030A   J            JOIN(PF1 PF2)
00040A                JFLD(EMPN EMPN)
00050A                EMPN JREF(1)
00060A                ADDR1
00070A                RATE
```

PF1 is the primary file and PF2 is a secondary file. Let us assume that PF1 and PF2 have the following records:

```
PF1                              PF2
EMPN   ADDR1                     EMPN   RATE
Beny   120 Sea St.              Beny   5.00
Dana   40 Doughley             Dana   2.50
Mike   2 Kackawax Dr.          Sura   5.50
Sura   120 Beltway
```

With JDFTVAL specified in the join logical file, the program reads the following records (shown in arrival sequence):

```
EMPN   ADDR1                   RATE
Beny   120 Sea St.            5.00
Dana   40 Doughley           2.50
Mike   2 Kackawax Dr.        0.00
Sura   120 Beltway           5.50
```

Without JDFTVAL specified in the join logical file, the program can read only three records (no record is found for Mike) The records would look as follows:

EMPN	ADDR1	RATE
Beny	120 Sea St.	5.00
Dana	40 Doughley	2.50
Sura	120 Beltway	5.50

Now, let's get a little ahead of ourselves to the JREF keyword which we generally explained above, and which we explain in detail below. In this example, if we specified JDFTVAL at the file level as well as JREF(2), instead of JREF(1) as originally specified, the field level for EMPN would be blank since that is the default for an unmatched secondary. The records returned to the program would be different, then, as follows:

EMPN	ADDR1	RATE
Beny	120 Sea St.	5.00
Dana	40 Doughley	2.50
Mike	2 Kackawax Dr.	0.00
Sura	120 Beltway	5.50

JDUPSEQ

The Join Duplicate Sequence keyword is available in join logical files only You would use this join-level keyword to specify the order in which records with duplicate join fields are presented when your program reads through a join logical file.

The format of the keyword is:

JDUPSEQ(sequencing-field-name [*DESCEND])

This keyword has no effect on the ordering of unique records. If you do not specify the keyword, the database does not guarantee the order in which records with duplicate join fields are presented, through the view. If you use more than one JDUPSEQ keyword in one join specification, the order in which you specify the JDUPSEQ keywords determines the order of presentation of duplicate records. This is similar to specifying an additional key field, in that it determines the order in which records with duplicate keys are presented.

Example

The following example shows how to specify the JDUPSEQ keyword.

```
00010A R JREC    JFILE(PF1 PF2)
00020A J JOIN    (PF1 PF2)
00030A          JFLD(EMPN1 EMPN2)
00040A          JDUPSEQ(PHON#)
00050A    EMPN1
00060A    ADDR1
00070A    PHON#
```

This example assumes that PF1 and PF2 have the following records:

```
PF1                    PF2
EMPN1 ADDR1            EMPN2 PHON#
BENY  120 Sea St.     BENY  555-1111
Doug  40 Doughley     BENY  555-6666
Mike  2 Kackawax Dr.  BENY  555-2222
                      Doug  555-5555
```

There are three records for BENY in PF2, showing three different telephone numbers. Notice that the JDUPSEQ keyword only affects the order of records when duplicates exist. With JDUPSEQ specified as shown, the records are returned as follows:

```
EMPN1       ADDR1          PHON#
BENY        120 Sea St.    555-1111
BENY        120 Sea St.    555-2222
BENY        120 Sea St.    555-6666
Doug        40 Doughley    555-5555
```

JFILE

The Joined Files keyword is for join logical files only, and it is specified at the Record Level. You would use this keyword to identify the physical files containing the data to be accessed through the join logical file you are in the process of defining.

The format of the keyword is:

JFILE([library-name/]physical-file-name [..32])

This keyword is specified, exactly as the PFILE keyword. The difference between the two is that the JFILE keyword identifies this file as a join logical file. The underlying physicals for the join logical file are specified in the JFILE as if the JFILE were the PFILE statement. There is no PFILE statement in a Join. Moreover, the JFILE keyword is not allowed with the PFILE keyword. If you have no JFILE keyword at the record level in your join logical file DDS, you will not create a join logical file.

One more difference with the PFILE is that the JFILE keyword requires a minimum of two physical file names. PFILE can have one or more names. You can also specify the same file name more than once, and we have an example coming up in a while which does just that with the EARNMAST file.

The first file specified in DDS is called the primary file. This is the file from which the join will begin. All other files are called secondary files. Even the third file is called a secondary file. Up to 31 secondary files can be specified . . . all the way up to 32 total files on one JFILE keyword.
Example 1

The following example shows how to specify the JFILE keyword.

```
00010A   R JRCD1R  JFILE(PF1 PF2)
00020A   J         JOIN(PF1 PF2)
00030A             JFLD(EMPN1 EMPN2)
```

In the join logical file, PF1 is the primary file and PF2 is the secondary file. This is an inner join. If there is not a match with the secondary, neither the primary nor the secondary record parts are in the view.

Example 2 - Join More Than Two Files

```
00010A R JRCD1R   JFILE(HELLO/PHYS1 +
00020A            HELLO/PHYS2 +
00025A            HELLO/PHYS3)
00030A J          JOIN(1 2)
00040A            JFLD(FIELD1 FIELD2)
00050A J          JOIN(1 3)
00060A            JFLD(FIELD1 FIELD2)
```

In the join logical file in Example 2, file PHYS1 in library HELLO is the primary file. File PHYS2 in library HELLO and file PHYS3, also in library HELLO are secondary files. Notice that there are three files in this join, and the functions area does not really give a lot of room to string things out — so we use three lines of DDS.

Instead of using the file names on the Join specifications, the example uses the numeric nomenclature in the JOIN statement to represent the file numbers in the sequence they were defined with the JFILE keyword. Thus, the Join level and JFLD keywords at statements 00030 and 00040 says to join File 1 with file 2 — a.k.a. PHYS1 with PHYS2. This adds the fields from File 2 to the join record. The next pair of JOINs and JFLDs (00050 and 00060) says to then join File 1 with File 3. This join picks up some fields from File 3. File 3, of course is PHYS3.

JFLD

The join level Joined Fields (JFLD) keyword is for join logical files only. You would use this keyword to identify the from and to fields, whose values are used to join physical files in a join logical file. JOINs and JFLDs are always specified in pairs. These fields are both referred to as join fields.

The format of the keyword is:

JFLD(from-field-name to-field-name)

If you do not specify a JOIN keyword, then the JFILE keyword is used to provide JOIN functionality. At least one JFLD keyword is required for each join specification. A join specification is identified by the "J" in position 17. Since at least one join specification is required in a join logical file, you must also have at least one JFLD keyword specified in a join logical file.

Unlike key fields which must be projected, the fields used These JFLD fields do not have to be projected. IN other words, they need not also be specified as fields in the record format for a join logical file. To specify additional join fields to use when joining physical files, you would simply use more than one JFLD keyword.

As you would expect from your study of DDS so far, the field names you specify on the JFLD keyword must either be specified at the field level in the join record format or in one of the physical files, as specified on the JFILE keyword.

Example

The following examples show how to specify the JFLD keyword.

Example 1:

```
00010A R JRCD1R JFILE(PF1 PF2)
00020A J       JOIN(PF1 PF2)
00030A         JFLD(EMPN1 EMPN2)
```

The fields used for the link in this simple join is the EMPN1
field in PF1 and the EMPN2 field in PF2.

JOIN

The Join keyword is for join logical files only and is specified at
the join level. You would use this join-level keyword to identify
which pair of files are joined by the JOIN specification in which
you specify this keyword.

The format of the keyword is:

JOIN(from-file to-file)

You can use file names or their relative file numbers to indicate
which files are to be joined. You must specify a relative file
number if the same file is specified more than once on the
JFILE keyword.

If you specify file names, you must select files that you have
specified only once on the JFILE keyword. In other words if
you ae joining a file to itself, you must use the relative file
number format on the JOIN rather than the file name.

To describe a join specification do the following:

1. Specify J in position 17 immediately after the record
    level (before the first field name in positions 19 through

28). The "J" in position 17 indicates the beginning of a join specification.

2. Specify the JOIN keyword. The JOIN keyword is optional when only two files are specified on the JFILE

JFILE is one of those keywords for which there are a lot of rules. They are not even all boring. It is also one of the keywords in which understanding the rules, can help you understand the keyword. Let's list some of these rules now:

1. On each JFILE keyword, the from-file must occur before the to-file.

2. If you specify numbers, they correspond to the files specified on the JFILE keyword. The following are the valid values:

File Valid Values

```
From-file number            To-file number
1 through 31                2 through 32
```

The from-file number must always be less than the to-file number. Rules continued:

1. In a join logical file, each secondary file can be a to-file only once.

2. When more than two physical files are specified on the JFILE keyword, one JOIN keyword is required for each secondary file.

3. Specify the JFLD keyword at least once for each join specification.

4. The end of the join specification is indicated by another J in position 17 or by a field name specified in positions 19 through 28.

5. There must be one join specification for each secondary file specified on the JFILE keyword. Therefore, at least one join specification is required in a join logical file. You can specify the JOIN keyword only once within a join specification.

Example 1

```
00010A R REC1      JFILE(PF1 PF2 PF3)
00020A J           JOIN(PF1 PF2)
00030A             JFLD(EMPN1 EMPN2)
00040A J           JOIN(PF1 PF3)
00050A             JFLD(EMPN1 EMPN3)
00060A    EMPN1
```

In this example, PF1 is joined to PF2 and also to PF3.

Example 2

The following example shows how to specify JOIN using relative file numbers.

```
00010A R RECORD1   JFILE(PF1 PF2 PF3)
00020A J           JOIN(1 2)
00030A             JFLD(EMPN1 EMPN2)
00040A J           JOIN(1 3)
00050A             JFLD(EMPN1 EMPN3)
00060A    EMPN1
```

Example 2 is equivalent to Example 1. PF1 is the first physical file specified on the JFILE keyword and has relative file number 1. PF2 and PF3 are the second and third files specified on the JFILE keyword and have relative file numbers 2 and 3, respectively.

JREF

The Join Reference keyword is specified at the field-level and is valid for join logical files only. Use this keyword in join logical files for fields whose names are specified in more than one physical file. With this keyword, you specify from which physical file, the values shown in the view should be taken.

The format of the keyword is:

JREF(file-Name | relative-file-number)

When using the JREF keyword, you can opt. to use the physical file name or its relative file number. If a physical file is named twice on the JFILE keyword, however, then you must specify the relative file number. There would be no other unique value. The relative file number corresponds to the physical file name specified on the JFILE keyword. For example, specifying JREF(1) associates a field with the first physical file specified on the JFILE keyword. Specifying JREF(2) associates a field with the second physical file specified on the JFILE keyword.

We have learned that Join logical files are based on two or more physical files (up to 32). The field names, which are specified in the record format in a join logical file, must uniquely identify at least one field from the physical files upon which the join logical file is based. For example, if the join logical file is built over two physical files, and each physical file has the field named EMPN, you must give the database a clue as to which EMPN are you talking about. Is it the EMPN in PF1 or the EMPN in PF2? To do this, you must specify the JREF keyword to identify from which physical file the duplicate fields in the logical format are to come.

When a field name is unique among the physical files specified on the JFILE keyword, there is no need to specify this JREF keyword. You can provide the keyword, however. It doesn't help or hurt. For example, if the join logical file is associated with two physical files, and only one of the physical files has an EMPN field, you do not need to specify the JREF keyword.

If the join logical file is associated with only one physical file (the JFILE keyword names the same file twice), you must specify the JREF keyword on every field since every field would exist twice.

Example 1

The following examples show how to specify the JREF keyword.

```
00010A R JRCD1R        JFILE(PF1 PF2 PF3)
00020A ...
00030A ...
00040A ...
00045  ...
00050A   EMPN          JREF(PF2)
```

In this example, the JREF keyword is specified with the file name, and EMPN occurs in both PF1 and PF2. Specifying JREF (PF2) associates this field with PF2.

Example 2

The following example shows how to use the file reference numbers to specify JREF.

```
00010A R JOINREC JFILE(PFA PFB PFC)
00020A :
00030A :
00040A :
00050A     EMPN      JREF(2)
```

Example 2 is equivalent to example 1. In example 2, EMPN occurs in both PFA and PFB. Specifying JREF(2) associates this field with PFB (the second of the physical files specified on the JFILE keyword).

Chapter 17   Logical File Coding Examples - Join Operations

The JOIN Relational Operator

A picture is worth a thousand words. Let's first take a look at the files which we are about to join in Figure F-38. Then, we'll let's code the DDS to make this type of join happen when we create the Join Logical File Object.

LF Data Diagram- Inner Join

In the simple join diagram shown in Figure F-38, rather than just use the part number in the order master, as you can see, the diagram shows how the description from the Parts master file is Joined into the corresponding records of the order master, The coding for this is in Figure F-39.

Figure F-38 Joining Data - Inner Join

```
ORDER Transaction                              PARTS   Master
|-----------|--------|-------|           |--------|-------------|-----|
|Order No   |Part No |Date   |           |Part No |Description  |Loc  |
|-----------|--------|-------|           |--------□-------------□-----|
|159244     |55511   |7/1/88 |           |55511   |CKK Valve    |Whs 1|
|           |        |       |           |        |             |     |
|263255     |29999   |7/7/88 |           |29999   |Left Bracket |Whs 3|
|           |        |       |           |        |             |     |
|978121     |64444   |6/9/88 |           |97676   |Brass plate  |Whs 1|
|           |        |       |           |        |             |     |
|. . .      |. . .   |. . .  |           |. . .   |. . .        |. . .|
*-----------!--------!-------E           *--------!-------------!-----E
            V                                     V
             V                                     V
              V                                     V
                         JOINED FILE
              |-----------|---------|------------------|
              |Order No   |Part No  |Description        |
              |-----------□---------□------------------|
              |159244     |55511    |CKK Valve          |
              |           |         |                   |
              |263255     |29999    |Left bracket       |
              |           |         |                   |
              |           |         |                   |
              |. . .      |. . .    |. . .              |
              *-----------!---------!------------------E
```

As you may deduce, the order number is the primary key of the
ORDER transaction file. Most of the other fields are not
shown. Part No is the primary key to the PARTS Master file.
Most of the other fields in the PART Master File are not
shown. The extra fields in both files are there for the ride and
need not be visible for this to work. They are not necessary for
the join we have diagramed

The objective of this exercise is to place the description field
into the matching ORDER Transaction records to create a
more human-readable record. The description exists only in the
PARTS master file. You can see how the joined record which
contains both the order information and the description, as
shown at the bottom of the diagram, has far greater utility for a
user than either file by itself.

Since Part No is a common field in both files, it will be used as
the linking field in the coding for the Join. The part number
field in the ORDER file has a one to one relationship with the
part record in the PARTS file. In other words, there is one
record, and only one record in the Parts Master file for each

record (Part No) in the ORDER file. There are no missing parts records. Of course we need information besides the shape of the data to know this as a fact. Since we know that the records in the ORDER Transaction file were edited at Order Entry time to assure that the part record exists for each part ordered, we know that there are no records in the transaction file that do not have a matching Parts record.

Therefore, we have the makings of what is called a natural join, or an inner join, or a matched join, or an equality join. In relation to the primary file (top left in the diagram and first file – left file – specified in DDS), there are no unmatched secondaries. Each transaction record points to an existing PARTS master record.

If, by any chance, there were a problem and there was a missing PARTS record for an ORDER record, the Equality join would not include any ORDER Transaction record in the logical view that was unmatched with a PARTS record.

LF DDS Coding Example - Inner Join

Figure F-39 LF Coding Joining Data - Inner Join

```
A* Logical FILE (INNER)
A*
A   R  INNERR          JFILE(ORDER PARTS)
    J                  JOIN(ORDER PARTS)
                       JFLD(PARTNO PARTNO)
       ORDNO
       PARTNO          JREF(ORDER)
       DESCR
    K  ORDNO
```

You can see in Figure F-39, the convention for naming the file within DDS comments – INNER. This example DDS represents a logical file join of the order file and the parts file as first shown in Figure F-38. There is a new record format

(INNERR) which consists of two fields from the ORDER file and one field from the PARTS file. It uses the logical file name plus "R" convention.

A Join view cannot be exactly the same as the structure of the primary physical file. Thus all Join views are projections. Joins are different because the projected fields come from more than one file.

Figure F-39 is the coding to get the inner join job done. Working from file to fields, the first file level keyword you see that you have never seen before is the JFILE keyword. JFILE is used to specify the file names which are being joined - in this case, ORDER, and PARTS. You may choose to qualify the file names if you do not anticipate the proper libraries being in the library list.

How are they to be joined? This question is answered by the JOIN parameter in conjunction with the JFLD parameter. The purpose of the JOIN parameter comes into play when there are more than two files to be joined. In fact, with just two files, you do not need the JOIN keyword at all. JFILE and JFLD are enough.

You use the JOIN record level parameter to identify the sequences of pairs for joining. In the above example, we tell the system to join ORDER to PARTS using the PARTNO fields from each file. It looks like the JFILE would serve this purpose just fine. However, the JFILE cannot do the trick when there is more than one join. For two, joins, you need two JOIN statements. For three joins, you need three JOIN statements, and so on until you reach 31 joins with 32 files. The notion of more than one Join is explored in the example shown in Figure F-43.

Since there is a PARTNO field in both files, you must tell the DDS which PARTNO field you want displayed in the joined record. Of course, they will have the same value when there is a match but will not if there is an unmatched record. The JREF(ORDER) statement accomplishes this.

Notice that there is a completely new format created with this view. Fields which you want in the view must all be specified. There is no option to take all fields in coding for a JOIN. In this format, two fields come from one file when there is a match and the part description comes from the other file.

Finally, notice that there is a key field on the join. This field orders the records so that they appear in a certain sequence in the view. There are some restrictions as to which fields can be key fields. For example, a key field must be projected in the view, and the field must come from the primary file.

Only when there is a match will a join record be included in the view. No Record appears for 978121 in Figure F-38, because there is no matching Parts record.

LF Data Diagram- Left Outer Join

The sample diagram in Figure F-40 depicts a Left Outer Join. In this join, as you can see, if there is no match with the primary (First file in JFILE) the system still includes the record in the view. However, since it has no field value from the secondary record, it assigns default values to the fields which would have come from the secondary file. In the chart in Figure F-40, you will notice that the unmatched records from the left file are included. This occurs because the JDFTVAL keyword (use join default values) was used at the file level in DDS.

Figure F-40 Left Outer Join (Default Join)

```
ORDER  MASTER                            PARTS  MASTER
|-----------|--------|-------|           |--------|-------------|-----|
|Order No   |Part No |Date   |           |Part No |Description  |Loc  |
|-----------|--------|-------|           |--------□-------------□-----|
|159244     |55511   |7/1/88 |           |55511   |CKK Valve    |Whs 1|
|           |        |       |           |        |             |     |
|263255     |29999   |7/7/88 |           |29999   |Left Bracket |Whs 3|
|           |        |       |           |        |             |     |
|970121     |64444   |6/9/88 |           |97676   |Brass plate  |Whs 1|
|. . .      |. . .   |. . .  |           |. . .   |. . .        |. . .|
*-----------!--------!-------E           *--------!-------------!-----E
            V                                     V
          V                                     V
        V                                     V
                      JOINED FILE
            |-----------|---------|------------------|
            |Order No   |Part No  |Description       |
            |-----------□---------□------------------|
            |159244     |55511    |CKK Valve         |
            |           |         |                  |
            |263255     |29999    |Left bracket      |
            |           |         |                  |
            |970121     |64444    |bbbbbbbb          |
            *-----------!---------!------------------E
```

As you can see in Figure F-40, the missing fields are filled with blanks if character. If numeric, the fields will be filled with zeroes and if the DFT keyword is used, the value specified for this default field will be used.

LF DDS Coding Example - Left Outer Join (Default Values)

The coding for the left outer join is shown in Figure F-41. As you can see the only difference between the coding in Figure F-39 and Figure F-41 is that the JDFTVAL is specified which makes the join a left outer Jon rather than an inner join.

Figure F-41 Coding DDS Logical File -Left Outer Join

```
A* Logical FILE (LOUTER)
A*
A                       JDFTVAL
A     R LOUTERR         JFILE(ORDER PARTS)
      J                 JOIN(ORDER PARTS)
                        JFLD(PARTNO PARTNO)
        ORDNO
        PARTNO          JREF(ORDER)
        DESCR
      K ORDNO
```

You can see in Figure F-41, the convention for naming the file within DDS comments – LOUTER. This example DDS represents a logical file join of the order file and the parts file as first shown in Figure F-40. There is a new record format (LOUTERR) which consists of two fields from the ORDER file and one field from the PARTS file. It uses the logical file name plus "R" convention.

LF Data Diagram- Left Outer Join with Multiple Matched Secondaries

Things are going to get a little more hairy now to show the power of the join. Unfortunately, our data does not work as well in this next step. So, we will play with the data a little bit to make it work. Instead of the ORDNO/PARTNO to PARTNO relationship (basically a one to one relationship from the Orders file to the Parts file since an order would have only one record for a particular part number), we are about to code a one to many relationship. Therefore, we must reverse the relationship of the test data and establish the Parts file as the primary file. In this way, as you can see in Figure F-42, there can be more than one order for a particular part number. This gives parts to orders a one to many relationship.

Figure F-42 Multiple Matched Secondaries

```
                   PARTS   MASTER
|--------|-------------|-----|
|Part No |Description  |Loc  |
|--------□-------------□-----|
|55511   |CKK Valve    |Whs 1|
|        |             |     |
|29999   |Left Bracket |Whs 3|
|        |             |     |
|97676   |Brass plate  |Whs 1|
|. . .   |. . .        |. . .|
*-----------!--------!-------E
Join the other way  One to many

                                           ORDER MASTER

                        |-----------|--------|-------|
                        |Order No   |Part No |Date   |
                        |-----------|--------|-------|
                        |159244     |55511   |7/1/94 |
                        |           |        |       |
                        |263255     |29999   |7/7/94 |
                        |           |        |       |
                        |978121     |97676   |6/9/94 |
                        |           |        |       |
                      |984315     |97676   |7/21/94|
                        *-----------!--------!-------E
                V                           V
                        JOINED FILE
        |----------|---------|------------------|
        |PART NO   |ORDR NO  |Description       |
        |----------□---------□------------------|
        |29999     |263255   |Left bracket      |
        |          |         |                  |
        |55511     |159244   |CKK Valve         |
        |          |         |                  |
        |97676     |978121   |Brass Plate       |
        |          |         |                  |
        |97676     |984315   |Brass Plate       |
        *----------!---------!------------------|
```

LF DDS Coding Example - Left Outer Join with Multiple Matched Secondaries (JDUPSEQ)

The primary file records are repeated in the join file view when more than one matching secondary record exists. JDFTVAL in this case would produce even more records than shown in Figure F-42 where there are no matched secondaries. The sequence in which the matching secondaries are retrieved is indeterminate unless you code the JDUPSEQ parameter as in Figure F-43.

Figure F-43 Coding Multiple Matched Secondaries -**JDUPSEQ**

```
A* Logical FILE (LOUTERM)
A                        JDFTVAL
A   R  LOUTERMR          JFILE(PARTS ORDER)
    J                    JOIN(PARTS ORDER)
                         JFLD(PARTNO PARTNO)
A                        JDUPSEQ(ORDNO)
       PARTNO            JREF(PARTS)
       ORDNO
       DESCR
    K  ORDNO
```

You can see in Figure F-43, the convention for naming the file within DDS comments – LOUTERM. This example DDS represents a logical file join of the PARTS file and the ORDER file as first shown in Figure F-42. There is a new record format (LOUTERMR) which consists of two fields from the ORDER file and one field from the PARTS file. It uses the logical file name plus "R" convention.

Other than the sequence of the file being changed (PARTS primary, ORDER secondary), the DDS is basically the same. However, there is one new keyword used in this example.

When you have multiple secondaries, there is another join specification (JDUPSEQ) which helps you assure that the matched or unmatched (JDFTVAL) secondary records will be presented in a defined sequence. In Figure F-43, look for the JDUPSEQ keyword. It is a JOIN level keyword and within the one parameter, the field name ORDNO is specified. The statement is repeated below for amplification:

A   **JDUPSEQ(ORDNO)**

In this case, JDUPSEQ tells the database to order the duplicates on ORDNO whenever there is a part number that is on more than one order, the JDUPSEQ gets the ORDER records virtually "sorted" in order number sequence, rather than random sequence. It tells the system to sort the orders in ascending sequence. If you coded the following, the database would present the multiple secondaries (duplicate order records) in descending sequence:

```
A        JDUPSEQ(ORDNO *DESCEND)
```

LF DDS Coding Example - Left Outer Join with Multiple Matched Secondaries Using Relative File Number

Figure F-44 demonstrates an alternate coding technique to that shown in Figure F-43. There is one difference in function but it is not caused by the alternate coding technique. We squeezed in another teaching opportunity.

Figure F-44 Alternate JOIN Coding Technique
```
A* Logical FILE (ALTJOIN)
A                              JDFTVAL
A      R ALTJOINR             JFILE(PARTS ORDER)
       J               □       JOIN(1 2)
                               JFLD(PARTNO PARTNO)
                               JDUPSEQ(ORDNO)
         PARTNO □ N             JREF(1)
         ORDNO
         DESCR
       K ORDNO
```

You can see in Figure F-44, the convention for naming the file within DDS comments – ALTJOIN. This example DDS represents a logical file join of the PARTS file and the ORDER file as first shown in Figure F-42. There is a new record format (ALTJOINR) which consists of two fields from the ORDER file and one field from the PARTS file. It uses the logical file name plus "R" convention. Though PARTNO seems to be included in this record format, check out the N code in the usage column. We'll get back to that.

The big thing in this example is the use of the relative file
number instead of the file name on many of the join keywords.
Instead of saying to specifically join PARTS to ORDERS, there
is another convention. You can use the relative sequence of the
file as specified on the JFILE statement. Thus, the DDS JOIN
records specification shows:

JOIN(1 2)

This says that File 1 is being joined to file 2. There is no
difference in function with this coding technique. Once fields
are defined with the JFILE, you can use numeric references for
them. This is a better coding technique, since the join files can
later change and the coding you have done with keywords does
not have to change.

The "N" specified in the Usage column tells the DDS compiler
that this join field will not appear in the join record. Thus, with
this coding, PARTNO is omitted from the resulting join
because of usage "N" Two Brass Plates are in the joined file
because of 2 matches, but the "N" has kept the PART NO field
from appearing in the resulting view.

LF Data Diagram- Three File Join

Figure F-45 Adding a Customer File - 3 Join Files

```
                    PARTS   MASTER
|--------|-------------|-----|
|Part No |Description  |Loc  |
|--------□-------------□-----|
|55511   |CKK Valve    |Whs 1|
|        |             |     |
|29999   |Left Bracket |Whs 3|
|        |             |     |
|97676   |Brass plate  |Whs 1|
|. . .   |. . .        |. . .|
*------------!--------!-------E
Join the other way  One to many


        ORDER / CUST                                    ORDER

|-----------|-------------|          |-----------|--------|-------|
| Order No  | Cust Name   |          |Order No   |Part No |Date   |
|-----------|-------------|          |-----------|--------|-------|
| 159244    | Ward's Store|          |159244     |55511   |7/1/94 |
|-----------|-------------|          |           |        |       |
                                     |263255     |29999   |7/7/94 |
                                     |           |        |       |
                                     |978121     |97676   |6/9/94 |
                                     |           |        |       |
                                     |984315     |97676   |7/21/94|
                                     *-----------!--------!-------E
                          V                          V
                 JOINED FILE
         |---------|------------------|-------------|
         |ORDR NO  |Description        | Cust Name   |
         |---------□------------------|-------------|
         |159244   |CKK Valve         | Ward's Store|
         |         |                  |             |
```

Now, let's add a customer file to this two-file set that we have been joining so well. As you can see in Figure F-45, this join will be very similar to those we have done in the past. More than likely, we will have multiple secondaries. In this case, we want an inner join so that only records with matches are selected. Thus, for each part in the PARTNO file, we only show the record if there is an order outstanding and if we have the customer link properly accommodated. By now, we know that the mere absence of the JDFTVAL keyword gives us a no default join.

Additionally, if we have an order record for a part, then we want to look up the customer name using another join. As you

will see in the DDS, there are two JOIN keywords in the DDS
because there are two joins as a data requirement.

LF DDS Coding Example - Three File Inner Join

Let's see how we might be inclined to code this. Look at
Figure F-46.

Figure F-46 LF Coding for Double Join

```
A* Logical FILE (DOUBJOIN)
A*
A
A     R   DOUBJOINR       JFILE(PARTS ORDER CUST)
      J                   JOIN(PARTS ORDER)
                          JFLD(PARTNO PARTNO)
      J                   JOIN(ORDER CUSTORD)
                          JFLD(ORDNO ORDNO)
          ORDNO
          PARTNO          JREF(PARTS)
          DESCR
          CUSNAM

      K   ORDNO
```

You can see in Figure F-46, the convention for naming the file
within DDS comments – DOUBJOIN. This example DDS
represents a logical file join of the PARTS file and the ORDER
file, joined again with the CUST file as first shown in Figure F-
45. There is a new record format (DOUBJOINR) which
consists of two fields from the ORDER file, one field from the
PARTS file, and one field from the CUST file. The example
uses the logical file name plus "R" convention.

OK, you've had enough time. But, go ahead and recheck the
coding in Figure F-46. Do you see anything wrong with this?
Are the join files OK? Are the key fields OK? What can be
wrong? Is nothing wrong?

Here are the Hints.

Now it's answer time. There are lots of things wrong with this coding.

1. The JFILE specifies a third file named CUST, yet this is not used by the JOIN statements. Instead a file named CUSTORD is used.

2. A joined view cannot be sorted on a secondary file. ORDNO is an invalid key the way it is positioned. You would need to make the order file the primary file in order to accomplish this.

3. PARTNO will be included in the view in this coding. To get it out, you would have to code an "N" in the DDS usage column on the line in which PARTNO is defined in the format.

4. There is no real way that you can link to the CUSTOMER file from the order file because no customer file ever designed would have order number within it.

5. However, there is a file called CUSTORD which has the customer name within it. This file can be part of the second join so that the objectives can be accomplished. The diagram in Figure F-45 shows the data in the CUSTORD file, including the customer name.

**LF DDS Coding Example - Corrected Three File Inner Join
The resulting corrected DDS would look like the example in
Figure F-46A**

Figure F-46A Corrected LF Coding for Double Join

```
A* Logical FILE (DOUBJOIN)
A*
A
A  R  DOUBJOINR     JFILE(ORDER PARTS CUSTORD)
   J                JOIN(ORDER PARTS)
                    JFLD(PARTNO PARTNO)
   J                JOIN(ORDER CUSTORD)
                    JFLD(ORDNO ORDNO)
      ORDNO
      PARTNO        JREF(PARTS)
      DESCR
      CUSNAM
   K  ORDNO
```

LF DDS Coding Example - Join File to Itself

There are lots of tricks that can be done with Join logical files.
If you can appreciate how they are done, then you will have a
better understanding of coding database files even if you do no
tricks. In the example in Figure F-47, we join a file to itself.
Hang on to your seats for this one.

Figure F-47 Join a File To Itself

```
A* Logical FILE (JOINSELF)
A*
A
A R  JOINSELFR        JFILE(EARNMAST EARNMAST)
   J                  JOIN(1 2)
                      JFLD(EMPNO MGRNO)
     EMPNO            JREF(1)
     EMPNAM           JREF(1)

     MGRNAM           JREF(2)
                      RENAME(EMPNAM)
     MGRNO            JREF(1)
   K EMPNO
```

You can see in Figure F-47, the convention for naming the file within DDS comments – JOINSELF. This example DDS represents a logical file join of the EARNMAST file with itself (EARNMAST). The record format name is built from the file name with the logical file name plus "R" convention.

There is a new record format (JOINSELFR) which consists of three fields from the primary file version of the EARNMAST and one field from the secondary file version of the EARNMAST file. You can tell the versions in the coding because the JREFs had to be coded to get the proper data in the record when the file was joined to itself.

Assume the objective is to have a view of the payroll data which includes the following fields: employee number, employee name, manager name and manager number. The problem is that there is no manager file. Yet each manager is an employee and each employee record includes manager number. So, theoretically, if after reading a record, you could tell the system to use the manager's number and go read the manager's record with the manager's employee number as the key, and you could store the manager's name in a different field, you can solve this problem.

The coding in Figure F-47 does exactly that. Though all of this data is in the same file, the manager name is in a different record. By using the JREF keyword on the EMPNAM and MGRNAM fields, the MGRNAM field gets populated when the secondary record (manager's employee record) is read to form the second half of the two file join. Since EMPNAM is renamed to MGRNAM, at the time of the secondary read, the EMPNAM field is different from what it was for the primary (employee) record read. Since the JREF is also used on all of the other fields in the primary file, the data does not get wiped out when the secondary record with the same fields is read. Thus the necessary managers' data is captured and presented in the view.

Notice in Figure F-47 that the EMPNO field is the designated join field for the primary file and the MGRNO field is the designated field for the secondary file. In fact, the primary file and the secondary file are one and the same, but the secondary read gets the manager's record, and this coding stores it successfully in the MGRNAM field.

Join Summary

Before we forget this stuff, let's summarize what we now know about a join.

1. Only One record format allowed

2. 1 to 32 joined physical files

3. Key fields must exist in a primary file

4. Secondary files must be joined in the same order as specified on the JFILE statement

5. Join files cannot be updated

Join is one of the most powerful operators in a relational database. If you have a good feeling for the DDS Join examples we examined in this chapter, you are well on your way to database proficiency with the AS/400 and IBM i. If you would like to explore SQL a little more, you are also in a better position to understand what this database language standard can do for you.

Chapter 18   Dynamic Record Selection - DYNSLT

DYNSLT Overview

You would use the DYNSLT file-level keyword to indicate that the selection and omission tests specified in the file (using select/omit specifications) are done at processing time. Technically, what this keyword tells the database is to use dynamic select/omit logic when the file is being processed rather than to continually maintain the access path with select/omit logic. Using DYNSLT, the cost (disk and processor) for the work involved by the database for the selection or omission of records is borne at the time the logical file (view) is used in a processing program. In other words if a program were reading the view sequentially, the determination of which records were presented (selected) and which records were not presented (omitted) would be done by the database while the program was reading records through the logical view.

Without DYNSLT, when the processing program opens the logical file, the access path already reflects the selections and there is no further burden on the database for the selection process. This true statement may make it seem that DYNSLT is a burden on the system and it should not be used. Actually, DYNSLT is often the most efficient way to process select /omit statements in a logical view even though it must first read each physical record to dynamically determine whether or not a record gets presented to the processing program.

In many ways the logic of DYNSLT is the same as if you had done no record selection in your logical view but, instead you did the selection / omission tests within your HLL program. However, since the DYNSLT work is done in the operating system, it is substantially faster than having to drag each record into your program, as required in the do-it yourself approach.

If the select/omit burden is not borne at processing time with DYNSLT, then it is borne continually as records are changed, added or deleted from the underlying physical file(s). There may be many programs which affect a file. For each change by any program the database would have to examine if the change affected the access path and if a record should be selected or omitted. Since the processing program has no part in this activity, the database makes the change to the access path itself. DYNSLT saves the system from all the checking and access path manipulation which would occur in a busy file. Without forcing the access path to be maintained for selections or omissions, the overall system performance for busy files is almost always better. If there were very few changes to the underlying data, then DYNSLT would not be as good an option for logical file processing.

DYNSLT Summary

As a program does input operations to a logical file with the DYNSLT keyword specified, all the records in the associated physical file are tested by the system to see if they satisfy the select/omit values. Only those records that satisfy the values are supplied to your program. It certainly costs the system at processing time to test each record and it can result in slower I/O performance, but it still may be more efficient than maintaining an access path for the file. This is particularly likely for files read only occasionally, especially when the physical files they are based on are updated frequently. Using dynamic select/omit is probably also more efficient for files with a high percentage of selected records.

☐ Hint: Though we have not yet covered logical file examples and keywords such as select/omit, and we have not shown join examples in this book, this information and the examples code which you see are provided at this time since the DYNSLT file level keyword is currently being studied. There is always a little chicken or the egg when introducing new material. You will better appreciate this arrangement when you use this book as a reference. If the notion of DYNSLT and select/omit is something you would prefer to deal with after you have digested the notion of logical files and select/omit logic, it is OK to skip or merely glance over this material at this time. But, we do expect you back!

When DYNSLT Does Not Apply

In keyed sequence access files, the system creates an access path at logical file creation time and the access path is maintained for the file according to the MAINT parameter on the Create Logical File (CRTLF) or Change Logical File (CHGLF) command. The DYNSLT keyword does not affect the maintenance of access paths for keyed sequence access files.

When DYNSLT Does Apply

For all single-format logical files with a DYNSLT keyword, you do not need to specify key fields in order to specify select/omit fields. However, for all multiple-format logical files with a DYNSLT keyword, you do need to specify at least one key field. The key field is used to bring them together. You can specify *NONE for this key field.

There are instances where you must do the record selection or omission dynamically using DYNSLT since the system does not always have an access path which easily accommodates select / omit logic. For example, you must use the DYNSLT keyword when you want to select or omit fields and any of the following conditions are true:

1. The logical file has an arrival sequence. The DDS in this case would have no key fields specified. This example is shown below as Example 1.

2. The logical file is a join logical file with the JDFTVAL (Join default value) keyword specified. You will come to learn the meaning of the JDFTVAL keyword very soon when we cover Join logical files. Basically it means that the primary file in a join will always present a record, even if the secondary file(s) has no matching record(s). The secondary data is provided as default values.

3. The logical file is a join logical file, and the select/omit fields come from more than one of the physical files the logical file is based on, and one of the following is also true:

   A. The select/omit fields are on the same select or omit statement. See example three below.

   B. The select/omit fields are on a mixture of select and omit statements. See example four below.

   C. The select/omit fields are on select statements that are ORed together.

   D. The select/omit fields are on omit statements that are ANDed together.

DYNSLT Examples:

The following four examples show how to specify the DYNSLT keyword in different circumstances.

Example 1:

The following example shows how to specify dynamic select with arrival sequence. Notice that there is no key field specified in the following DDS.

```
00010A                   DYNSLT
00020A    R RECORD1      PFILE(PF1)
00030A      FIELD1
00040A      FIELD2
00050A    S FIELD1       COMP(GT 2)
```

The PFILE keyword in statement 00020 is at the record level and it says that this record format is in the physical file named PF1. This is the keyword which tells the logical file which physical file(s) it is based upon. Statement 00050 is where the selection takes place. It reads like this: When FIELD1 is greater than 2, include the record in the view. The DYNSLT keyword is required because there are no key fields (K in column 17). The logical file applies dynamic selection and supplies the records to your program in arrival sequence. Assume that physical file PF1 has the following records:

```
FIELD1 FIELD2
  1      AAA
  2      XXX
  3      KKK
  4      BBB
```

As your program does input operations, the system tests the first two records according to the select/omit values, but does not supply them to your program since the value of FIELD1 is not greater than 2. Therefore, your program sees only the last two records:

FIELD1	FIELD2
3	KKK
4	BBB

Example 2

The following example shows how to specify dynamic selection when there is a keyed sequence access path.

```
00010A                    DYNSLT
00020A    R RECORD1       PFILE(PF1)
00030A                    FIELD1
00040A                    FIELD2
00050A    K FIELD1
00060A    S FIELD2        COMP(GT 'BBB')
```

In this example, the DYNSLT keyword is actually not required. The logical file supplies records to your program in keyed sequence. Let's assume that physical file PF1 has the following records:

FIELD1	FIELD2
1	AAA
2	XXX
3	KKK
4	BBB

When your program requests a record, the system tests the value of FIELD2 for that record according to the select/omit values. Therefore, your program only sees the following records:

FIELD1	FIELD2
2	XXX
3	KKK

Example 3

The following example shows you how to specify a join logical file using select/omit logic which compares fields from two different physical files.

```
00010A              DYNSLT
00020A   R REC1     JFILE(PF1 PF2)
00030A   J          JOIN(Pf1 PF2)
00035A              JFLD(FIELD1 FIELD3)
00040A     FIELD1   JREF(PF1)
00050A     FIELD2   JREF(PF1)
00060A     FIELD3   JREF(PF2)
00070A     FIELD4   JREF(PF2)
00080A   S FIELD1   COMP(GT FLD4)
```

This example uses a join. There are four keywords necessary for a join. The JFILE (join file) keyword in 00020 says that files PF1 and PF2 will be joined. The "J" or join record (column 17) uses the JOIN (join files) keyword to specify the order in which the files are being joined. This can be different from the order in the JFILE. The JFLD (join field) keyword in statement 0035 shows which fields are being joined - Field1 is in PF1, and FIELD3 is in PF2.. The next keyword is the JREF (join reference file) and this tells the DDS compiler when two files being joined have the same field names, which file to take the data from.

FIELD1 and FIELD2 come from the primary file (PF1). The primary file is the first file specified in a join, and FIELD3 and FIELD4 come from the secondary file (PF2). The select specification compares FIELD1 from the primary file with FIELD4 from the secondary file. Therefore, the DYNSLT keyword is required. See Rule 3A above.

Example 4

The following example shows how to specify a join logical file that contains both select and omit statements which come from more than one physical file.

```
00010A              DYNSLT
00020A R JREC       JFILE(PF1 PF2)
00030A J            JOIN(PF1 PF2)
00040A              JFLD(FIELD1 FIELD2)
00050A    FIELD1    JREF(PF1)
00060A    FIELD2    JREF(PF1)
00070A    FIELD3    JREF(PF2)
00080A K FIELD1
00090A S FIELD1    COMP(GT 0)
00100A O FIELD3    COMP(GT 4)
```

FIELD1 and FIELD3 come from different physical files and are specified in a mixture of select and omit statements. Therefore, the DYNSLT keyword is required according to rule 3B above.

Chapter 19   Date and Time Formats

Many Operations Use Date and Time

This book would be incomplete if we did not give some attention to the data and time formats. I would suggest reading the material in IBM's Physical and Logical File Database Guide which you can find by using the Appendix of this book. Many operations use the date or the time as a critical value. We know that from the effort expended in the Y2K battle that dates are very important. Yet, many of us continue to use our own hand-written code to handle date routines, rather than using the database field type and using the various date and time formatting facilities available in DDS.

There are three special data types that the DDS formatting keywords apply to. Moreover, the length for fields with data type L (date), T (time), or Z (timestamp) is determined by the system. When defining such a field in DDS, you are told specifically by IBM not to enter a field length in positions 30 through 34 of the DDS specification. IBM believes you don't have to know the internal format as long as there is a way for you to externalize the date and date-like fields in one or many pleasing formats. Additionally, being the multi-language company IBM is, you can bet they can take those crazy shaped fields and make them look like any type of date that you need. If you think this, you are absolutely correct!

Let's take a look in reasonable detail about the date formats and date separator keywords and we'll use this as a basis for leveraging a discussion on the other formats. In other words, if they are basically the same, you would probably [refer that we say that, rather than present everything two or three times, and let you figure it out. Let's start with the DATFMT keyword.

DATFMT

The Date Format keyword is valid for both physical and logical files. You would use this keyword to specify the format of a date field. This keyword is valid only for date fields (data type L) or for logical file zoned fields (data type S), packed fields (data type P), or character fields (data type A) whose corresponding physical file fields are date fields (data type L). Already you know that the date separator can deal with more than IBM's internal date format.

The format of the keyword is:

DATFMT(date-format)

It would not be too much to suggest that the date-format keyword specifies the format for the date. That is exactly what it does. IBM has built a table that is printed in the Physical and Logical Files Database Guide which describes the valid date formats and their default separator values for physical file fields. Let's examine this table in Figure F-48

Figure F-48 Date Format Table

```
Format Name       Date-
Format
Parameter         Date Format
and
Separator
          Field
Length  Example
Job Default       *JOB
Month/Day/Year    *MDY    mm/dd/yy        8        06/23/69
Day/Month/Year    *DMY    dd/mm/yy        8        23/06/69
Year/Month/Day    *YMD    yy/mm/dd        8        69/06/23
Julian  *JUL      yy/ddd  6       69/174
International
Standards Organization   *ISO    yyyy-mm-dd      10      1969-06-23
IBM USA Standard         *USA    mm/dd/yyyy      10      06/23/1969
IBM European Standard    *EUR    dd.mm.yyyy      10      23.06.1969
Japanese Industrial
Standard Christian Era   *JIS    yyyy-mm-dd      10      1969-06-23
```

1. Other attributes of the DATFMT keyword for physical file fields are:

2. You may specify only the DATFMT keyword on the date (L) data type.

3. If you do not specify the DATFMT keyword, the default is *ISO.

4. Field length values and decimal position values must be blank.

The IBM i DDS Reference: Physical and Logical Files manual which is in IBM's Web Library (access instructions in the Appendix) has a very large table of supported formats and separations for logical files. You may want to take a trip to this manual if you have a project where detailed knowledge of dates is key to the solution.

Example

The following example shows how to specify the DATFMT keyword.

```
00010A R RECORD
00020A    DATE1    L    DATFMT(*JUL)
00030A    DATE2    L    DATFMT(*EUR)
```

If the current date is June 23, 1969, the current system date format value is MDY, and the current system separator is /, DATF1 contains 90/172 (the 174th day of the year 1969). DATE2 contains 21.06.1990.

DATSEP

The Date Separator keyword is for both physical and logical files. You would use this field-level keyword to specify the separator character for a date field. This keyword is valid only for date fields (data type L).

The format of the keyword is:

DATSEP(*JOB | 'date-separator')

The date separator parameter specifies the separator character that appears between the year, month, and day. Valid values are a slash (/), dash (–), period (.), comma (,) or blank ( ). The parameter must be enclosed in apostrophes.

If you specify *JOB, the default is the job attribute. For physical files, if you do not specify the DATSEP keyword, the default is the job attribute. For logical files, if you do not specify the DATSEP keyword, the default is the date separator from the physical file. If you did not specify the DATSEP keyword for the physical file field (*ISO, *USA, *EUR, or *JIS was specified on the DATFMT keyword), the default for DATSEP is the job attribute.

If you specify the *ISO, *USA, *EUR, or *JIS date format value on the DATFMT keyword, you cannot specify the DATSEP keyword. These formats have a fixed date separator. The DATSEP keyword overrides the job attribute. It does not change the system default.

Here is an Example:

The following example shows how to specify the DATSEP keyword.

```
00020A R RCD1R
00030A   DATE3 L  DATFMT(*DMY) DATSEP('-')
00040A   DATE4 L  DATSEP(' ')
```

If the current date is June 23, 1969, the current system date format value is MDY, and the system date separator value is '/', DATE3 contains 23-06-69. DATE4 contains 06 23 69.

Time and Timestamp Operations

The Keywords for time and timestamp are as follows:

TIMFMT (Time Format)

TIMSEP (Time Separator)

The IBM i DDS Reference: Physical and Logical Files manual which is in IBM's Web Library (access instructions in the Appendix) has a table of supported time formats and separations for physical logical files. You may want to take a trip to this manual if you have a project where detailed knowledge of time fields is key to the solution.

Chapter 20   Summary and Conclusions

Data Base Summary

In this mini course, we examined native database coding on the AS/400 and IBM i. We answered the following questions along the way:

1. What is a data base?
2. Why is a data base needed?
3. What is the AS/400 data base?
4. How does one use the AS/400 data base for data creation / manipulation?
5. How do you code DDS for Physical and Logical Files

This course has defined what a data base is, explained the benefits of having an integrated data base on a data processing system, and it introduced the AS/400 integrated, relational data base and followed up with a series of highly useable examples. You should now be prepared to move off and begin making more effective use of this marvelous database tool

It's now time to go have some database fun!

Our best wishes for your database future!

LETS GO PUBLISH! Books by Brian Kelly:

(Sold at www.bookhawkers.com; Amazon.com, and Kindle.).

LETS GO PUBLISH! is proud to announce that more AS/400 and Power i books are becoming available to help you inexpensively address your AS/400 and Power i education and training needs: Our general titles precede specific AS/400 and other technology books. Check out these great patriotic books which precede the tech books in the list.

Seniors, Social Security & the Minimum Wage
The impact of the minimum wage on Social Security Beneficiaries

How to Write Your First Book and Publish It With CreateSpace
This books teaches how to create a book with MSWord and then publish it with CreateSpace. No need to find a traditional publisher.

Healthcare & Welfare Accountability The Trump Way
Why should somebody win the Lottery & not pay back welfare?

The Trump Plan Solves Student Debt Crisis. .
This is the Trump solution for new student debt and the existing $1.3 Trillion student debt accumulation.

Take the Train to Myrtle Beach The Trump Way.
Tells all about the Donald Trump Plan to restart private passenger railway systems in America while it tells you how to get to Myrtle Beach by Train.

RRRRRR The Trump Way.
This book represents the overarching theme of the Trump campaign with verbs ready to reign in the excessive policies of the Obama Administration. These are the six verbs for the RRRRRR plan: Reduce, Repeal, Reindustrialize, Raise, Revitalize, Remember

Jobs! Jobs! Jobs! The Trump Way!
All about the jobs mess we ae in along with a set of Trump solutions

The Trump Plan Solves the Student Debt Crisis
Solution for new student debt and the existing $1.3 Trillion debt accumulation

101 Secrets How to be a High Information Voter
You do not have to be a low-information voter.

Why Trump?
You Already Know… But, this book will tell you anyway

Saving America The Trump Way!
A book that tells you how President Donald Trump will help America so that Americans wind up on top

The US Immigration Fix
It's all in here. Finally an answer to the 60 million interlopers in America. You won't want to put this book down

I had a Dream IBM Could be #1 Again
The title is self-explanatory

Whatever Happened to the IBM AS /400?
The question is answered in this new book.

Great Moments in Penn State Football
Check out the particulars of this great book at bookhawkers.com.

Great Moments in Notre Dame Football
Check out the particulars of this great book at bookhawkers.com or www.notredamebooks.com

WineDiets.Com Presents The Wine Diet
Learn how to lose weight while having fun. Four specific diets and some great anecdotes fill this book with fun and the opportunity to lose weight in the process.

Wilkes-Barre, PA; Return to Glory
Wilkes-Barre City's return to glory begins with dreams and ideas. Along with plans and actions, this equals leadership.

The Annual Guest Plan.
This is a plan which if deployed today would immediately solve the problem of 60 million illegal aliens in the United States.

Geoffrey Parsons' Epoch... The Land of Fair Play
Better than the original. The greatest re-mastering of the greatest book ever written on American Civics. It was built for all Americans as the best govt. design in the history of the world.

The Bill of Rights 4 Dummmies!
This is the best book to learn about your rights. Be the first, to have a "Rights Fest" on your block. You will win for sure!

Sol Bloom's Epoch ...Story of the Constitution
This work by Sol Bloom was written to commemorate the Sesquicentennial celebration of the Constitution. It has been remastered by Lets Go Publish! – An excellent read!

The Constitution 4 Dummmies!
This is the best book to learn about the Constitution. Learn all about the fundamental laws of America.

America for Dummmies!
All Americans should read to learn about this great country.

Just Say No to Chris Christie for President two editions – I & II -- Discusses the reasons why Chris Christie is a poor choice for US President

The Federalist Papers by Hamilton, Jay, Madison w/ intro by Brian Kelly
Complete unabridged, easier to read, annotated version of the original Federalist Papers

Companion to Federalist Papers by Hamilton, Jay, Madison w/ intro by Brian Kelly
This small, inexpensive book will help you navigate the Federalist Papers

Kill the Republican Party!
2013 edition and edition #2)
Demonstrates why the Republican Party must be abandoned by conservatives

Bring On the American Party!
Demonstrates how conservatives can be free from the party of wimps by starting its own national party called the American Party.

No Amnesty! No Way!
In addition to describing the issue in detail, this book also offers a real solution.

Saving America
This how-to book is about saving our country using strong mercantilist principles. These same principles that helped the country from its founding.

RRR:
A unique plan for economic recovery and job creation

Kill the EPA
The EPA seems to hate mankind and love nature. They are also making it tough for asthmatics to breathe and for those with malaria to live. It's time they go.

Obama's Seven Deadly Sins.
In the Obama Presidency, there are many concerns about the long-term prospects and sustainability of the country. We examine each of the President's seven deadliest sins in detail, offering warnings and a number of solutions. Be careful. Book may nudge you to move to Canada or Europe.

Taxation Without Representation Second Edition
At the time of the Boston Tea Party, there was no representation. Now, there is no representation again but there are "representatives."

Healthcare & Welfare Accountability
Who should pay for your healthcare? Whose healthcare should you pay for? Is it a lifetime free ride on others or should those once in need of help have to pay it back when their lives improve?

Jobs! Jobs! Jobs!
Where have all the American Jobs gone and how can we get them back?

Other IBM I Technical Books

The All Everything Operating System:
Story about IBM's finest operating system; its facilities; how it came to be.

The All-Everything Machine
Story about IBM's finest computer server.

Chip Wars
The story of ongoing wars between Intel and AMD and upcoming wars between Intel and IBM. Book may cause you to buy / sell somebody's stock.

Can the AS/400 Survive IBM?
Exciting book about the AS/400 in a System i5 World.

The IBM i Pocket SQL Guide.
Complete Pocket Guide to SQL as implemented on System i5. A must have for SQL developers new to System i5. It is very compact yet very comprehensive and it is example driven. Written in a part tutorial and part reference style, Tons of SQL coding samples, from the simple to the sublime.

The IBM i Pocket Query Guide.
If you have been spending money for years educating your Query users, and you find you are still spending, or you've given up, this book is right for you. This one QuikCourse covers all Query options.

The IBM I Pocket RPG & RPG IV Guide.
Comprehensive RPG & RPGIV Textbook -- Over 900 pages. This is the one RPG book to have if you are not having more than one. All areas of the language covered smartly in a convenient sized book Annotated PowerPoint's available for self-study (extra fee for self-study package)

The IBM I RPG Tutorial and Lab Guide
Your guide to a hands-on Lab experience. Contains CD with Lab exercises and PowerPoint's. Great companion to the above textbook or can be used as a standalone for student Labs or tutorial purposes

The AS/400 & IBM i Pocket Developers' Guide.
Comprehensive Pocket Guide to all of the AS/400 and System i5 development tools - DFU, SDA, etc. You'll also get a big bonus with chapters on Architecture, Work Management, and Subfile Coding. This book was updated in 2016..

The IBM i Pocket Database Guide.
Complete Pocket Guide to System i5 integrated relational database (DB2/400) – physical and logical files and DB operations - Union, Projection, Join, etc. Written in a part tutorial and part reference style. Tons of DDS coding samples.

Getting Started with The WebSphere Development Studio Client for System i5 (WDSc).
Focus is on client server and the Web. Includes CODE/400, VisualAge RPG, CGI, WebFacing, and WebSphere Studio. Case study continues from the Interactive Book.

The System i5 Pocket WebFacing Primer.
This book gets you started immediately with WebFacing. A sample case study is used as the basis for a conversion to WebFacing. Interactive 5250 application is WebFaced in a case study form before your eyes.

Getting Started with WebSphere Express Server for IBM i
Step-by-Step Guide for Setting up Express Servers
A comprehensive guide to setting up and using WebSphere Express. It is filled with examples, and structured in a tutorial fashion for easy learning.

The WebFacing Application Design & Development Guide:
Step by Step Guide to designing green screen IBM i apps for the Web. Both a systems design guide and a developers guide. Book helps you understand how to design and develop Web applications using regular RPG or COBOL programs.

The System i5 Express Web Implementer's Guide. Your one stop guide to ordering, installing, fixing, configuring, and using WebSphere Express, Apache, WebFacing, System i5 Access for Web, and HATS/LE.

Joomla! Technical Books

Best Damn Joomla Tutorial Ever
Learn Joomla! By example.

Best Damn Joomla Intranet Tutorial Ever
This book is the only book that shows you how to use Joomla on a corporate intranet.

Best Damn Joomla Template Tutorial Ever
This book teaches you step-by step how to work with templates in Joomla!

Best Damn Joomla Installation Guide Ever
Teaches you how to install Joomla! On all major platforms besides IBM i.

Best Damn Blueprint for Building Your Own Corporate Intranet.
This excellent timeless book helps you design a corporate intranet for any platform while using Joomla as its basis.
4
IBM i PHP & MySQL Installation & Operations Guide
How to install and operate Joomla! on the IBM i Platform

IBM i PHP & MySQL Programmers Guide
How to write SQL programs for IBM i

Joomla! books and many of the tech books above are only available at www.bookhawkers.com. Most books are available at amazon.com, Kindle, and other fine booksellers online and in the stores.